Only Guide You Need - Things to Do in Retirement

Simple Steps to Discover New Passions, Boost Health, & Build Social Connections to Thrive in Your Newfound Freedom

Patti Gomas

Contents

Introduction

As you step into the uncharted territory of retirement, a thrilling new adventure awaits. No more meetings or office politics. Now, you have the freedom to explore, discover, and redefine what brings you joy and purpose. But with this freedom comes a common question: "What will your next great adventure be?"

Retirement is a blank canvas, ready for you to paint with vibrant colors and bold strokes. It's a chance to rediscover passions, nurture your well-being, and forge meaningful connections with others. However, many retirees find themselves unsure of where to begin, feeling a bit lost in this new chapter of life.

That's where this book comes in. Consider it your trusty compass, guiding you through the uncharted waters of retirement. This book is not just a source of inspiration but a practical guide. It provides specific ideas and activities tailored to various budgets and locations, ensuring there's something for everyone. It's like having a personal coach ready to help you thrive in this new chapter of life. Please don't feel obligated to read it from cover to cover but rather flip through it often and stop at the sections that interest you most. This book is part of a series and a second volume setup in a similar way will be coming soon with even more suggestions for crafting the best retirement ever.

I initially wrote this to celebrate my parents' retirement milestone. During my research, I realized I wanted to retire sooner. As a result, I decided to work with a financial advisor to create an updated retirement plan that would allow me to reach this exciting stage of life earlier.

Through this process, I also discovered the challenges that new retirees often face. It's common to experience a loss of purpose or feelings of isolation after leaving the workforce. You may find yourself wondering how to fill the seemingly endless hours ahead of you. But don't worry; this book is designed to help you combat boredom and rediscover the joy of trying new things.

Throughout these pages, you'll discover actionable ideas to enhance your lifestyle and redefine your purpose. We will focus on meaningful activities that promote personal growth, improve your health, and strengthen social connections. Each chapter concludes with easy-to-follow action steps, allowing you to implement these ideas right away.

I've poured my passion for helping retirees into this book, drawing from my own experiences and the stories of those I've met. I've seen firsthand how embracing new adventures and building a strong support network can transform retirement into the most fulfilling years of one's life.

It's important to note that **this book <u>isn't</u> about financial planning or management**. While those topics are certainly important, our focus here is on lifestyle, personal growth, and creating a retirement that brings you joy and satisfaction.

As we explore various aspects of retirement, including health-boosting activities and ways to stay socially connected, you'll find a variety of ideas to suit your interests. Whether you're an adventurous spirit eager to explore new horizons or a creative soul looking to dive into new hobbies, there's something here for you.

So, are you ready to embark on this exciting new chapter? To discover hidden passions, build meaningful relationships, and create a retirement that exceeds your wildest dreams? Then, let's get started.

Remember, the possibilities are endless. With this book as your guide and a spirit of curiosity, you have the power to make these years the most rewarding and fulfilling of your life. Get ready to embrace the adventure, my friend. Your next great chapter starts now.

CHAPTER ONE

Finding Your Spark

Have you ever watched a sunrise after a long, restful sleep? The sky gradually shifts from a deep indigo to a spectrum of vibrant hues, each moment more breathtaking than the last. This daily wonder reminds us that beginnings are beautiful and full of promise and potential. Retirement can be much like that sunrise, marking the start of a new day in your life, where the possibilities are as endless as the sky. So, what will your new dawn bring?

Retirement is often seen as the end of an era, but it's far from a conclusion. Instead, it's a beginning, an open invitation to rediscover who you are beyond the work you've done. Many people face this transition with a mix of excitement and apprehension. There's the lure of freedom, yet also the fear of losing a sense of purpose that a career often provides. But what if you could view retirement as your "second act," a chance to redefine yourself and explore new horizons? This chapter is about transforming any anxieties you may have into opportunities for growth and adventure. It's about stepping into this new phase with confidence, ready to embrace all the potential it holds.

A Fresh Start: Embrace Your New Adventure

Retirement is not an end but a new beginning, a blank page for you to fill with fresh stories and adventures. This fresh start presents a unique opportunity to reimagine your life and focus on the activities and connections that truly matter to you.

Take this time to reflect on what you want to achieve in the coming years and how you wish to spend your days. Whether it's traveling to destinations you've always dreamed of, pursuing a hobby you never had time for, or simply enjoying the little things that bring you joy, this is your moment to shine.

It's normal to feel a bit lost at first, unsure of how to redefine your identity outside the workforce. The idea of losing the structure and responsibility that work provides can be daunting, leading to a sense of disorientation or even anxiety. You might wonder, "Who am I now?" or "What is my purpose?" These are natural questions, ones that many have wrestled with. But remember, the end of a career is not the end of your story. It's an opportunity to write new chapters full of discovery and excitement.

Consider using powerful tools like vision boards and journaling to help guide you through this transition. These aren't just activities; they're exercises in self-discovery and goal-setting.

A vision board, for instance, is more than just cutting pictures from magazines. It's a tangible way to visualize your aspirations, a daily reminder of what you're striving for. Place it somewhere you'll see it often, and let it inspire you to take steps toward the life you envision. According to *Conservatory*

Senior Living, a well-crafted vision board can help you clarify your retirement goals, such as health, travel, and community involvement, making them feel more attainable and tangible.

Journaling, on the other hand, allows you to reflect deeply on your thoughts and feelings. It's a private space where you can explore what truly makes you happy and document your journey as you navigate this new domain. Whether you're writing about your dreams, recounting the day's events, or penning down what you're grateful for, the act of putting pen to paper can bring clarity and peace. It's a simple yet powerful way to connect with your inner self and track your growth over time.

Goal setting is another crucial element of this fresh start. By setting SMART goals — Specific, Measurable, Achievable, Relevant, and Time-bound — you can create a structured plan to achieve what you've always dreamed of. Whether it's learning a new language, volunteering for a cause close to your heart, or mastering a musical instrument, setting clear goals can provide direction and motivation. As noted by _Hebrew SeniorLife_, having a purpose linked to structured goals can significantly enhance happiness and vitality during retirement.

Remember, this phase of life is about embracing change, not fearing it. The social pressures and misconceptions about aging can sometimes make us doubt our abilities. However, this chapter aims to reassure you that it's never too late to start anew. Many retirees have found joy and fulfillment by stepping outside their comfort zones, trying things they never thought possible, and proving that age is just a number. Embrace change, and let it be the fuel for your new adventures.

So, as we venture on this path together, know that you're not alone. Each page of this book is designed to support you, offering practical advice and encouraging stories from those who have walked this path before you. Together, let's shed any doubts and replace them with excitement. Let's turn the page and begin this new adventure with open hearts and open minds. The sky is the limit, and your best days are yet to come.

Creating a Life You're Excited to Live

Imagine waking up each morning with a sense of anticipation, eager to embrace the day's adventures. That's the power of having a clear purpose in retirement, a guiding light that illuminates the path ahead. At the heart of this newfound direction is the vision board — a simple yet profound tool designed to help you visualize your retirement aspirations. Think of it as a personalized roadmap filled with the destinations and experiences you dream of. A vision board serves as both a reminder of your goals and a source of inspiration, nudging you to turn dreams into reality. It's like having a compass that always points toward your north star, ensuring you stay on course even when life gets busy.

Creating a vision board is a joyful and creative process. Start by gathering materials that resonate with your soul. Old magazines are treasure troves of images and words that might speak to your heart. You can also explore digital resources like Canva or Pinterest, which offer endless possibilities for crafting a virtual masterpiece.

As you sift through images, let your imagination run wild. Look for pictures that capture your ideal experiences—whether it's a serene beach, a bustling cityscape, or a cozy kitchen filled with laughter. Add words and quotes that inspire you and echo your deepest desires and aspirations. This is about crafting something deeply personal, a visual representation of what you want your life to look like.

Once you have your materials, it's time to assemble your board. Choose a space in your home that feels right, where you'll encounter it daily. It could be the wall by your breakfast nook or next to your favorite reading chair. If you are creating a digital vision board, use it as your computer, tablet, or mobile wallpaper.

The key is visibility. Each glance should remind you of what you're working toward and why it matters. This isn't just art; it's a living document that evolves with you. As your interests and goals shift, so too should your vision board. Consider setting aside time each month to revisit it. Are there new dreams you want to add? Goals that need tweaking? This ritual keeps your aspirations fresh and aligned with your evolving self.

Vision Board Creation Checklist:

- **Materials Needed**: Magazines, printouts, scissors, glue, a poster board, or digital tools like Canva or Pinterest.

- **Visualize Your Goals**: Select images and words that represent your dreams and aspirations.

- **Designate a Space**: Hang or place your vision board where you see it daily (kitchen and mobile phone wallpaper are top choices).

- **Involve Loved Ones**: Share the experience with family or friends for added support.

Creating a vision board can be done either as a personal reflection exercise or as a group activity. Invite family or friends to join you in this creative endeavor. Their perspectives can enrich your vision, offering insights you might not have considered. Plus, sharing your goals with loved ones fosters accountability and support. They become your cheerleaders, encouraging you to pursue the life you envision. This shared experience can deepen bonds and create lasting memories, making the process as rewarding as the outcome.

A vision board is simply a collage of images and words that speak to your soul and align with what you want next in life. There are no rules to your vision board. It's personal to you and can be broad, covering your life dreams or specific themes like travel or health goals. You can create multiple boards and put them throughout your home. You can create various digital wallpapers (a quick Google search can provide a ton of templates perfect for exactly your device) that you can swap out as often as you like.

Remember, a vision board is not static. It should grow and change as you do. Life is dynamic, and your aspirations will evolve. Regularly revisiting your board ensures it remains a true reflection of your dreams. This practice keeps you motivated and focused, and it is a gentle reminder of what you're striving for. It's about aligning your daily actions with your overarching goals, creating a life that excites and fulfills you.

As you embark on this process, embrace the possibilities that lie ahead. Let your vision board be a testament to your dreams, a canvas on which you paint your future. With each image and word, you're not just imagining a life you love — you're taking steps to make it a reality. Your journey has just begun, and the possibilities are as vast and varied as your imagination allows.

Journaling Your True Purpose

In the quiet moments of reflection, a simple pen and paper can become powerful allies. Consider journaling as a tool not just for recording daily events but for unlocking the deeper layers of who you are and what you desire. Journaling invites you to pause and sift through the noise of everyday life, allowing your thoughts to take shape and your purpose to become apparent. It's a practice where you can articulate your dreams, track your progress, and gain the mental clarity needed to navigate this new phase of life.

Imagine starting (or ending) your day by jotting down a few things you're grateful for. This simple act of recording daily gratitude can shift your mindset, encouraging you to notice the small joys that might otherwise go unnoticed. Whether it's the warmth of a morning cup of coffee, the laughter shared with a friend, or the serene beauty of a sunset, acknowledging these moments can cultivate a positive outlook and enrich your daily life. Gratitude journaling is not about grand gestures but about celebrating the little things that make life meaningful.

For those who enjoy a bit of structure, reflective prompts can guide your thoughts and help uncover insights into your past accomplishments and future aspirations. Questions like "What did I enjoy most about my career?" or "What legacy do I want to leave?" can open doors to self-discovery and help you connect with your core values and desires. These prompts act as gentle nudges, encouraging you to explore paths you may not have considered and to rekindle passions that may have been set aside during your working years.

There are various styles of journaling, each offering a unique way to express yourself. Stream-of-consciousness writing, for instance, allows you to write freely without concern for grammar or structure. It's about letting the words flow naturally, revealing subconscious thoughts and emotions that might otherwise remain hidden. This form of writing can be liberating, offering a window into your innermost self. Guided journaling, on the other hand, provides specific prompts that encourage focused reflection, offering an opportunity to delve deeper into topics that matter to you.

Visual journaling is another creative approach that combines words and images to express your thoughts. By incorporating sketches, collages, or photographs, you can add a visual dimension to your reflections, making the process more engaging and personal. This method can be particularly effective for those who find that images speak louder than words, allowing you to capture the essence of your experiences in a way that resonates deeply.

Of course, like any practice, journaling can have its challenges. Writer's block is a common hurdle, where the blank page feels daunting, and words seem elusive. If you find yourself stuck, try changing your environment or starting with a simple list of what's on your mind.

There are a ton of printed journals for any journaling desire.

<u>Here are some of my favorite searches on Amazon (or whatever is your favorite retailer):</u>

- Gratitude journaling

- Reflective journaling

- Travel journaling

- Bullet journaling

- Art journaling

- Mood journaling

- Stream-of-consciousness journaling

If you want to go digital with your journaling, these three apps are fantastic. For Windows/Android users, try **Diarium**. For Mac/iOS users, try **Day One**. **Grid Diary** is available on both app marketplaces and is excellent for templated journaling.

Another strategy is to join a journaling circle, where you can share your entries with others and gain fresh perspectives. Discussing your reflections with trusted friends can offer motivation and inspire new insights, enriching the journaling experience.

Journaling is not about perfection or producing polished prose. It's a personal dialogue, a space where you can explore your thoughts without judgment. It's about capturing moments of clarity and using them to guide your actions and decisions. As you continue this practice, your journal becomes a faithful companion, a testament to your growth, and a roadmap to your future. In this quiet yet profound way, journaling can help you reveal your true purpose and design a life that excites and fulfills you.

Turn Dreams into Reality

Imagine standing at the base of a tall mountain, its peak hidden among the clouds, representing the dreams you've held close for years. To reach them, you need a clear and steady path. SMART goals provide a structured approach to turning dreams into measurable accomplishments. SMART stands for Specific, Measurable, Achievable, Relevant, and Time-bound, a framework that can help shape your aspirations into realistic plans. Instead of vague resolutions that drift away, SMART goals anchor your intentions, providing clarity and direction.

Picture this: You've always wanted to learn a new language. Instead of simply deciding to "learn Spanish," a SMART goal would be to "attend a weekly Spanish class and practice for 30 minutes daily for six months." This goal is specific and measurable, with a clear timeline. Or consider volunteering. Rather than vaguely committing to "volunteer more," a SMART approach might be to "volunteer at the local food bank for four hours every Saturday for three months." These goals not only give you a clear target but also outline the steps to get there, making them achievable and relevant to your life.

In retirement, aligning your goals with your values becomes crucial. This phase of life is about what truly matters to you. It could be family, adventure, health, or leaving a legacy. Whatever it is, your goals should reflect these core values. If community involvement is important to you, your goals might focus on finding volunteer opportunities that allow you to connect and contribute. If health is a priority, setting goals around fitness or nutrition can keep you on track. The key is to ensure your goals resonate with what you hold dear, giving them more profound meaning and purpose.

Now, it should make more sense why we discussed vision boards and journaling before this step. If you did either of those activities, creating SMART goals is a snap. It's okay if you didn't do those things, but know that they are excellent ways to get the juices flowing.

Creating an action plan is the next step in turning these dreams into reality. Break down each goal into smaller, manageable milestones. Think of it as laying stepping stones across a stream; each one takes you closer to the other side. If your goal is to travel, start with small steps like researching destinations, setting a budget, and planning itineraries. Use tools like checklists or templates to track your progress. These can serve as visual reminders of your journey, keeping you motivated and focused on the finish line.

Celebrating milestones is vital. Recognize each small victory along the way. Rewarding yourself for achieving a milestone can reinforce your commitment and make the process enjoyable. It doesn't have to be elaborate — a simple treat or an evening with friends can suffice. The idea is to acknowledge your efforts and successes, building momentum as you continue forward. Keep your family and friends up to date on your progress so they can celebrate with you.

Life is unpredictable, and flexibility is essential. As you progress, new interests may emerge, or circumstances might change. Goals that once seemed critical might shift in priority. Regular reassessment allows you to adapt, ensuring your goals remain aligned with your current life and desires. Consider revisiting your goals every few months. Are they still relevant? Do they need adjusting? This adaptability ensures your goals remain a true reflection of your evolving self.

SMART goals create a strong foundation for a fulfilling retirement. It's about taking concrete steps toward the life you envision, one that resonates with your values and aspirations. With clarity, structure, and a willingness to adapt, you can transform your dreams into reality, making your retirement years genuinely extraordinary.

Becoming the You You've Always Wanted

In the transition from working life to retirement, many of us face the challenge of stepping away from the identities we've built over decades. Your career may have defined you in countless ways, providing structure, purpose, and a sense of belonging. Now, as you close that chapter, the absence of a title or routine can feel daunting. But this moment also holds immense potential. Retirement offers the freedom to explore who you are beyond your career and to redefine yourself in ways that resonate with your evolving interests and passions. It's a time to embrace new roles that might have seemed out of reach in the past.

Consider the stories of those who have walked this path before you. Consider the former finance executive who found joy in an unlikely place. After setting down his brief-case, he discovered a passion for pottery — a hobby he'd always admired but never pursued. With each spin of the wheel, he found solace and satisfaction, eventually turning his newfound love into a small business, selling beautifully crafted pieces at local markets. Another retiree, a lifelong educator, channeled her skills into mentoring young adults in her community, offering guidance and support as they navigated their own career paths. These stories of reinvention illustrate the endless possibilities that await when you open yourself to new experiences. The chapters ahead in this book will dive into the details of these ideas, but here's a little sample of what's to come.

One of the most rewarding aspects of this stage is the opportunity to engage in community life. Volunteering or mentoring can provide a fulfilling way to share your skills and wisdom with others. Imagine joining a local organization where you can contribute to meaningful projects, meet new people, and make a positive impact. Whether it's helping at a food bank, offering your expertise to a nonprofit, or mentoring young professionals, these roles can bring a renewed sense of purpose and connection. They remind us that our contributions matter and that we can still change lives and communities even after leaving the workforce.

Artistic pursuits also offer a rich avenue for exploration. Ever wanted to try your hand at painting, sculpture, or photography? Now is the perfect time. These creative outlets not only nurture the soul but also provide a platform for self-expression and growth. Local workshops and classes can be excellent places to start. They offer the chance to learn new skills, meet like-minded individuals, and participate in community fairs or exhibitions. Here, you can experiment, make mistakes, and celebrate successes in a supportive environment. By engaging in these activities, you not only enrich your own life but also contribute to a vibrant and diverse community culture.

Community involvement at this stage of life can significantly enhance your sense of belonging and fulfillment. Organizing or participating in neighborhood events is a great way to connect with those around you. Imagine hosting a small gathering, like a book club or potluck dinner, where neighbors can come together, share stories, and build friendships. These interactions create a network of support and camaraderie, making your community feel like an extension of your family. They offer both a platform for sharing your talents and an opportunity to learn from others.

Taking active roles in local events encourages a sense of empowerment. It allows you to contribute to the community's vibrancy and growth. You become an integral part of a larger tapestry, one where each thread enhances the whole. Through these engagements, you discover new facets of yourself, uncover hidden talents, and find joy in the collective achievements of the group. This stage of life is not just about personal fulfillment but also about leaving a positive mark on the world around you.

As you step into these fresh roles, remember that the possibilities are as varied as your interests. Whether you seek adventure, creativity, or the satisfaction of helping others, retirement offers a time to explore it all. This is your moment to become the person you've always wanted to be, to embrace the passions that have long awaited your attention. The world is rich with opportunities, and your unique journey is just beginning to unfold.

Crafting the Perfect Retirement Plan

Envisioning your best life in retirement requires more than just daydreaming. It's about deepening your self-reflection, understanding what truly brings you joy, and deciding what legacy you wish to leave behind. This process starts with a values inventory exercise. Imagine sitting quietly with a cup of tea, pondering what matters most to you. Is it family gatherings filled with laughter, the thrill of adventure, the pursuit of health, or the joy of contributing to your community? Identifying these core values is like finding the North Star that will guide your decisions and goals. Aligning your retirement plans with these values ensures that your actions resonate with your deepest desires, making every choice feel significant and purposeful.

Transforming your reflections into actionable plans can be jumpstarted by breaking these into long-term and short-term goal groups. Short-term goals include starting a new hobby or exploring nearby places you've always wanted to visit. These are the quick wins that bring immediate satisfaction and keep you motivated. Long-term aspirations involve more significant undertakings, like traveling the world or learning a complex skill. This is where the SMART goals framework becomes invaluable. By ensuring each goal is Specific, Measurable, Achievable, Relevant, and Time-bound, you create a clear path forward that's both realistic and inspiring. This approach transforms vague dreams into concrete plans, making them much easier to tackle and achieve.

To support this planning process, consider using goal-setting templates or apps. These act as guides, breaking down your long-term dreams into manageable steps. Think of them as blueprints for your aspirations, showing you precisely what needs to be done and when. They can help you track your progress, adjust your plans as needed, and celebrate your achievements along the way. There's something profoundly satisfying about ticking off a completed step on your journey toward a larger goal. It's a reminder that you're moving forward, no matter how slowly, and that progress is being made.

Here are some of my favorite goal-setting apps:

- *Todoist* - super easy interface and a variety of task management capabilities

- *Habitica* - this transforms your goal setting into a game with quests and rewards (my absolute favorite!)

- *Strides* - great customizable trackers for different goal types

- *GoalsOnTrack* - perfect for SMART goals and has some nice visual tools

Visualizing new roles, you might want to explore in retirement can also provide clarity. Perhaps you've always seen yourself as a traveler, roaming new countries with curiosity. Or the thought of mentoring young minds or volunteering for a cause close to your heart excites you. These roles are not just labels; they represent new chapters of your life where you can apply your skills and passions in meaningful ways. To help brainstorm these possibilities, try using an identity exploration worksheet. This tool encourages you to list your skills, interests, and potential roles you might enjoy. It's a way to connect the dots between who you are and who you want to become, opening doors to opportunities you may not have considered before.

PositivePschology.com has a great Who Am I worksheet (it's free). It asks questions like:

- How would your closest friend or family member describe you in one paragraph?

- If one of your coworkers were to tell a story about you, what do you think they would say?

- If your life partner were describing your biography, what kinds of things would they mention?

- If you were writing to your past self, what would you choose to include about who you are now?

- Imagine you're talking to your future self. What would you say about what makes you you?

Consider the case of a retiree who spent years in corporate management. Upon retiring, she realized her passion lay in teaching, something she had only dabbled in before. By reflecting on her skills and interests, she found a new role as a volunteer teacher at a local community center. This new identity not only rekindled her love for learning but also allowed her to make a positive impact in her community. It's a testament to the power of self-reflection and planning in crafting a fulfilling retirement.

Retirement is a period of life rich with potential, and planning is key to realizing this potential. It's about taking the time to reflect on what you want and need in this new chapter. Whether it's a small, immediate goal or a grand, long-term vision, each step forward is a step toward a life that is profoundly satisfying and true to who you are. So take this time to think, plan, and envision the life you've always wanted to live. The path is yours to create, and the possibilities are endless.

Wrap-Up: Embrace Retirement Freedom

Retirement is a time to dance to your own rhythm, to forge a path that reflects your dreams and aspirations, not just a passive lull in the timeline of life. Whether you choose to sail the seas of creativity, dive into community engagements, or savor the bliss of a morning without an alarm clock, it's a period ripe with potential. It's about taking charge and shaping this chapter with intention and enthusiasm. Too often, retirement is mistakenly viewed as an endpoint. In truth, it's the beginning of a new chapter where you hold the pen, writing a story rich with possibilities and joy. This is your chance to break free from the constraints of past routines and societal expectations to explore the uncharted territories of your interests and passions.

You might feel a flicker of hesitation, but remember, each small step you take can lead to monumental changes. Start with something simple, a tool or technique that resonates with you. It could be creating a vision board that captures the essence of what you want to achieve or setting a new goal that sparks excitement. The important thing is to start, no matter how modest the beginning may seem. Taking that first step is empowering; it's a declaration of your commitment to embrace all that life has to offer in this exciting phase.

Consider the possibilities that open before you. This is your time to experiment and explore hobbies, interests, and activities that spark joy. There's no rush and no right way to do it. The beauty of retirement is that it allows for flexibility and freedom, giving you the space to explore at your own pace.

You can redefine not just how you spend your time but how you perceive yourself and your place in the world. As you explore these new avenues, allow yourself the grace to pivot and adapt as your interests evolve.

It's easy to feel overwhelmed by the vastness of it all but remember, the best time to start is now. When you align your actions with your passions, the path forward becomes more apparent and more fulfilling. Let this be a call to action, an invitation to embrace the freedom that retirement offers. Say yes to the adventures that await, to the friendships you'll forge, and to the personal growth you'll experience.

As you continue to explore the possibilities of retirement, carry with you the knowledge that this is a time of empowerment. You are the author of this chapter, shaping it with each decision and action you take. So why not start today? Whether it's a small step or a giant leap, every move you make brings you closer to a retirement filled with purpose, joy, and fulfillment. Embrace this freedom, for it is yours to savor, and let it lead you to a life that genuinely reflects who you are and who you wish to become.

Your action item from this chapter is to DO any of the suggestions. Do one, do them all, it doesn't matter... start doing!

CHAPTER TWO

New Friends, New Adventures

P icture yourself at a bustling neighborhood block party, the air filled with laughter and the scent of food on the grills. As you sip your drink, you overhear snippets of stories from around the party — tales of recent travels, new-found hobbies, and cherished memories. It's a scene that embodies the heart of social connections, offering a variety of shared experiences and friendships. In retirement, this vibrant social network can become a cornerstone of your well-being, providing joy, companionship, and a sense of belonging. For many, the social aspect of life takes on new meaning during retirement. Without the automatic connections that work often provides, the search for meaningful interactions can feel daunting. You might find yourself wondering, "Where will I meet new friends?" or "How can I stay active and engaged?" The good news is the world is full of opportunities to build a rich social life. Through engaging in your community, you can develop new friendships that enhance your quality of life and open doors to fresh adventures.

Building Your Social Network

Social engagement is not just a luxury; it's a vital component of healthy aging. Meaningful interactions can enhance your mental, emotional, and physical well-being. Imagine joining a community theater group, where each rehearsal is an opportunity to step into a new role, not just on stage but in life. The camaraderie of working together toward a common goal promotes friendships that extend beyond the play. Similarly, participating in a local choir allows you to harmonize not only your voice but also your life with others, creating a melody of shared joy and connection. Community involvement combats isolation, offers a sense of purpose, and enriches your days with laughter and companionship. According to a study on social participation, engaging in community-based activities can significantly enhance life satisfaction and reduce feelings of loneliness. Whether it's volunteering at a local charity or joining a gardening club, these activities provide a platform for connection and fulfillment.

Staying active and engaged is about more than just filling your calendar; it's about keeping your mind sharp and your spirit lively. Consider the energy of a local cultural festival, where vibrant colors and lively music invite you to explore new traditions and form new friendships. Volunteering at such events not only allows you to give back but also presents chances to meet like-minded individuals who share your passion for cultural exploration. Or consider joining a hiking group that meets weekly to explore nearby trails and natural wonders. Each trek offers not just physical exercise but also moments of shared awe and discovery, strengthening bonds with fellow hikers.

As you embark on this journey of building your social network, consider reflecting on what truly excites you. What activities bring you joy? Is it the thrill of theater, the rhythm of music, or the tranquility of nature? Take a moment to jot down your thoughts. Consider the types of connections you value. Are you drawn to small, intimate gatherings, or do you thrive in larger, bustling groups? Reflecting on these questions can guide you toward activities and communities that align with your interests and enrich your retirement.

Page Turners & New Connections: Book Clubs

Imagine curling up with a good book, losing yourself in a riveting story, and then gathering with friends to discuss the twists and turns. Book clubs offer more than just reading; they provide a gateway to social engagement and intellectual stimulation. In a world where screens often dominate our attention, the tactile joy of turning pages and sharing insights with others can be profoundly satisfying. By discussing diverse perspectives, you open your mind to new ideas and experiences. Each meeting becomes an opportunity to delve deeper into themes and characters, fostering a sense of community and shared learning. The regularity of these gatherings establishes a comforting routine, a time to connect with others and enjoy a shared passion.

It's easy to join existing book clubs by contacting your local library, community center, or area university. However, starting your own book club can be as simple as reaching out to friends, neighbors, or even members of your community center. Begin by identifying individuals who share your love for literature, perhaps those you've exchanged book recommendations with in passing. Once you have a list of potential members, consider the ideal venue for your meetings. Libraries offer a quiet, literary atmosphere, while coffee shops bring a casual, social vibe. Community centers can provide the space needed for larger groups. Rotating hosting at members' homes is also a nice way to get to know people better.

Selecting the first book is crucial; aim for a universally appealing title that sparks interest and conversation. This book serves as the foundation, setting the tone for future discussions and ensuring everyone feels included.

Here are some tips to ensure a great book choice:

- **Familiar Genres:** Consider popular genres such as historical fiction, mysteries, biographies, and classics.

- **Large Print and Audio Options:** Let's face it. Our eyes and ears aren't working the way they used to. To accommodate everyone's abilities, prioritize books available in large print or audiobook format.

- **Shorter Length:** Opt for shorter books or novellas to respect varying attention spans and reading paces.

- **Nostalgia and Reminiscence:** Choose books that evoke memories or connect to past experiences to spark discussion. This also invites participation in the discussion even if members can't remember every plot twist.

- **Accessibility:** Select books that are readily available in libraries, bookstores, or online. Make it easy to participate.

Maintaining a successful book club requires planning and flexibility. Encourage members to take turns hosting or leading discussions, bringing fresh perspectives and ideas to each meeting. This rotation not only prevents burnout but also ensures that everyone feels a sense of ownership and investment in the group. Preparing discussion guides can enhance conversations, providing structure with thought-provoking questions or themes to explore. These guides act as a springboard for dialogue, ensuring that each member can share their thoughts and insights. By fostering an inclusive environment, you create a space where all voices are heard and valued.

Alternative formats offer flexibility and accessibility for those unable to meet in person. Online book clubs, using platforms like Zoom, allow members to connect from the comfort of their homes, breaking geographical or mobility barriers. These virtual gatherings can be just as engaging as their in-person counterparts, providing a platform for lively discussion and connection.

Themed book clubs offer another twist, focusing on specific genres or authors. Whether it's a mystery, historical fiction, or a beloved author, these themes provide a focused framework for exploration. By tailoring the format to suit your group's preferences, you create a dynamic and adaptable book club that meets the needs of its members. Be sure to get feedback from the group often about what they like and don't like. Keep trying new things and making it better. Remember, book choices can also be a way to help support members through tough times. A book about a character rebounding after the loss of a spouse or a difficult health diagnosis can be just what a member needs and an excellent way for the group to rally around that member.

Book clubs are not just about books; they're about connection, exploration, and the joy of shared experiences. They provide a space to engage with others, challenge your perspectives, and foster a lifelong love of reading. As you embark on this literary adventure, remember that the true magic of a book club lies in the friendships and insights gained along the way.

Spice Up Your Social Life: Cooking Classes

There's something magical about gathering around a table filled with dishes bursting with flavor and color. Cooking is not just about feeding the body; it's an art form, a way to express creativity and explore new cultures from the comfort of your kitchen. As you chop, stir, and taste, you're not only creating a meal but crafting an experience, one that can be shared with friends and family. Engaging in culinary exploration opens a world of diverse cuisines and cooking styles, each with its own story and technique. Whether you're mastering the delicate layers of a French croissant or the rich spices of an Indian curry, cooking offers endless possibilities to broaden your palate and skills. Moreover, it serves as a social bridge, bringing people together through shared culinary adventures. Imagine the laughter and camaraderie as you knead dough alongside fellow foodies or exchange secret family recipes during a potluck.

Finding the right cooking class to match your interests and skill level can be an exciting endeavor. Local culinary schools and community centers often offer a variety of courses, from beginner classes to advanced workshops, catering to different tastes and expertise levels. You might find your-self drawn to a class focusing on Mediterranean dishes one week and baking the next. These classes provide not only a structured learning environment but also a community of like-minded individuals eager to explore the culinary arts.

The easiest way to find classes near you is to do an online search:

- What specific local culinary schools or community centers offer cooking classes in different cuisines?

If in-person classes aren't feasible, virtual options abound, of-fering flexibility and convenience. Online platforms provide access to world-class chefs and specialized courses, allowing you to learn at your own pace from the comfort of your home. Whether you choose a local setting or a digital class-room, the opportunities to expand your culinary horizons are abundant.

Here are some of my go-to online cooking class providers (available live and on-demand so you can whisk up this adventure whenever the mood strikes):

- **Cozymeal:** Great selection of virtual cooking classes

taught by professional chefs. You can choose courses based on your interests, cuisine, and skill level.

- **Sur La Table:** Offers a wide variety of online cooking classes in different cuisines, from French pastries to Thai curries.

- **MasterClass:** Features online cooking classes taught by celebrity chefs and culinary experts, covering a wide range of cuisines and techniques.

- **YouTube:** Many chefs and food bloggers offer free cooking tutorials and demonstrations on YouTube. Search based on your interests and skill level. (From Julia to Man and A Can)

Beyond practical skills, cooking offers big benefits for personal growth. It's a creative outlet that encourages experimentation and fosters a sense of accomplishment. As you master new recipes and techniques, your confidence in the kitchen grows, empowering you to tackle more complex dishes with ease. In addition to honing your culinary prowess, these classes can enhance your nutritional knowledge, teaching you about healthy ingredients and meal preparation. Understanding the balance of flavors and nutrients can lead to healthier eating habits, enriching both your physical health and culinary enjoyment. The act of cooking becomes a journey of self-discovery, where each dish you create reveals something new about your tastes and abilities.

Consider the stories of those who've embraced cooking as a social and creative pastime. One retiree found immense joy in hosting themed dinner parties, where each meal became a celebration of a different culture. Friends gathered to savor dishes from around the world, sharing stories and experiences over a lovingly prepared feast. Another discovered a passion for culinary competitions, testing skills, and creativity in a fun, supportive environment. These experiences fostered friendships and provided a sense of community, all centered around a shared love of food. Cooking is much more than a means to an end. It's a way to connect with others, explore new worlds, and express who you are in the most delicious way possible. Bon Appetit!

Step Into the Spotlight: Join a Local Theater

Imagine stepping onto a stage, the lights warming your face, and the audience eagerly waiting to be delighted by you and your cast. Local theater offers a unique opportunity to explore the world of drama and performance, a realm where you can express creativity and dive into new personas. It's more than just acting; it's a chance to build confidence, improve communication, and engage in a collective storytelling experience. As you memorize lines and rehearse scenes, you develop skills that transcend the stage, enhancing your ability to communicate and express yourself confidently in everyday life. Theater is a transformative experience, one that encourages you to step outside your comfort zone and discover hidden talents.

Getting involved in community theater begins with finding a group that resonates with you. Local community centers and bulletin boards are great resources for discovering theater groups, or you can search for local community theaters on Google Maps, many of which welcome newcomers with open arms. The audition process, often seen as daunting, is simply a gateway to possibility. Auditions are a chance to showcase your personality and enthusiasm, regardless of prior experience. Preparation is key: understand the role, practice your lines, and approach the process with an open heart and mind. The excitement of being cast in a role is unmatched, setting the stage for new friendships and creative fulfillment.

However, theater is not confined to acting alone; there are numerous roles behind the scenes that are vital to a production's success. If you have a talent for organization or a passion for design, consider exploring stage management, technical, or production roles. Areas where your skills can shine include lighting, sound, costume design, and production management. These roles are the backbone of any performance, and they offer a chance to learn new skills and contribute in meaningful ways. The friendship built within a theater community is special. Each member plays a part in bringing a story to life, creating a shared sense of achievement and belonging.

Many retirees have found renewed purpose and joy through theater. Take, for instance, a retired teacher who found a second home in her local theater troupe. Initially drawn to set design, she gradually ventured into acting, discovering a talent she never knew existed. Each rehearsal was a new adventure filled with laughter, learning, and connection. Or consider the former engineer who applied his analytical skills to the technical aspects of theater, mastering lighting design and stage management. Both found not only a creative outlet but also a community of friends who shared their passion. These stories highlight the transformative power of theater as a space for personal growth and connection. In the words of Shakespeare, "All the world's a stage, and we are merely players."

The Sound of Friendship: Music and Choirs

Picture a room filled with voices blending in harmony, the air vibrating with the joy of shared melody. This is the magic of community music and choirs, where every note is sung and every chord struck joins a chorus of connection and joy. Whether you're joining a local choir or playing in an instrumental ensemble, making music together offers a profound emotional boost. The act of singing or playing music is therapeutic, a balm for the soul that can alleviate stress and elevate your mood. It's not just the music itself but the shared experience of creating something beautiful that brings people together, fostering unity and a deep sense of belonging.

Finding the right music group can transform your retirement into a time of creativity and connection. Local choirs and bands often welcome new members with open arms, and churches, community centers, and online platforms are excellent places to start your search. Many groups hold open rehearsals where you can get a feel for the ensemble and the types of music they perform. Auditions, in many cases, are informal and more about gauging your enthusiasm and commitment than technical skill. This welcoming environment provides a safe space to explore your musical abilities and connect with others who share your passion.

Finding Your Musical Niche:

1. **Online Search:** Start by doing a simple online search for "choirs near me" or "music groups near me." This will often lead you to the websites or social media pages of local ensembles.

2. **Community Hubs:** Check community centers, libraries, and places of worship. They often have bulletin boards or newsletters listing local groups.

3. **Local Music Stores:** Music stores are great places to find information about local music teachers, groups, and events. You can even start a new musical journey.

4. **Social Media:** Search Facebook groups or pages related to music in your town. You can find groups dedicated to specific genres or instruments.

5. **Meetup.com:** This platform often lists groups based on shared interests, including music.

6. **Nextdoor:** This social networking site for neighborhoods can help find music groups in your immediate area.

Music groups come in many flavors, each offering its own unique experience. If you have a love for classical music, joining a choir that performs timeless pieces by composers like Mozart or Beethoven could be deeply rewarding. For those who enjoy more contemporary sounds, some ensembles focus on modern hits, jazz standards, or even folk music. Instrumental groups, such as community bands or orchestras, offer musicians the chance to collaborate in creating rich, layered soundscapes. Whether you've played an instrument for years or are picking one up for the first time, these groups provide an inviting space to learn and grow.

Engaging with music in this way can lead to personal transformation. Many individuals find a renewed sense of purpose and confidence through their involvement in music. Take, for instance, the story of a retiree who, after years away from the piano, joined a local jazz ensemble. Each practice session was a step toward reclaiming a passion he'd nearly forgotten, and in doing so, he found friendship and fulfillment. Another member of a choir shared how the act of singing each week helped her navigate the challenges of retirement, providing a structured activity that brought joy and a sense of accomplishment. These stories illustrate the powerful impact of music, not just as an art form but as a means of connecting with yourself and others.

From Parades to Performances: Cultural Festivals

Imagine the vibrant colors of a street parade, the rhythmic pulse of drums echoing through the air, and the tantalizing aroma of eclectic foods drawing you in. Cultural festivals are more than just celebratory events; they're gateways into the heart of diverse traditions and communal joy. They offer a unique opportunity to immerse yourself in different cultures, learning about customs, art forms, and culinary delights that might be new to you. Each festival is a living tapestry of human expression, weaving together stories from around the world. As you wander through these events, you discover not only the richness of other cultures but also deepen your understanding of your own.

The festive atmosphere is infectious. People from all walks of life come together, united by a shared sense of wonder and celebration. The energy is vivid proof of human creativity and connection. Participating in these festivals can be an exhilarating way to meet new people and form friendships. Whether it's joining a traditional dance, sampling exotic dishes, or marveling at intricate crafts, each activity fosters a sense of community and belonging. It's a reminder that, despite our differences, we are all connected through shared experiences and the universal language of joy.

Getting involved in cultural festivals can be as simple as volunteering. Many events welcome helping hands to organize and run the festivities. By joining an event committee, you not only contribute to the success of the festival but also build new relationships. Working side by side with others toward a common goal forges friendships and creates a sense of camaraderie. Moreover, volunteering provides a behind-the-scenes look at what makes these festivals tick, offering insights into the meticulous planning and passion that bring them to life. It's a fulfilling way to give back and feel part of something larger than yourself.

Beyond volunteering, consider attending workshops and demonstrations offered during festivals. These sessions provide hands-on learning experiences that can expand your cultural knowledge and spark new interests. Imagine learning to make traditional crafts, cook authentic dishes, or dance to the beat of foreign rhythms. Each workshop is an opportunity to step outside your comfort zone and engage with the festival on a deeper level. It's a chance to learn directly from artisans and experts, gaining skills and insights that enrich your personal growth and understanding.

Hands-On Workshops at Cultural Festivals:

Many cultural festivals offer hands-on workshops and demonstrations. Some are so fantastic they may warrant a special trip (like Carnival in Rio de Janeiro, Brazil, The Festival of Colors in Holi, India, Mardi Gras in New Orleans, USA, or Oktoberfest in Munich, Germany). Here are a few examples of the types of activities that can be found at festivals:

- **Art workshops:** Learn how to create pottery, paint, or other forms of art.

- **Music workshops:** Learn how to play a musical instrument or sing in a choir.

- **Cultural dance workshops:** Learn traditional dances from different cultures.

- **Cooking demonstrations:** Learn how to prepare traditional dishes from different cultures.

- **Historical reenactments:** Get a glimpse into the past through interactive historical reenactments.

Cultural festivals come in many forms, each offering its unique flavor. From food and art festivals to film and music events, there's something for everyone. These gatherings celebrate not just diversity but also the creativity and expression that define us as human beings. Attending them opens doors to personal enrichment, allowing you to explore different facets of culture and art. It's a journey of discovery where you can appreciate the beauty and intricacy of human expression across the globe.

Consider the stories of those who have embraced cultural festivals to enrich their lives. One individual found new friends and a deeper appreciation for cultural diversity by regularly attending local events. Another discovered a passion for traditional dance after participating in a festival workshop, leading to ongoing classes and a newfound hobby. These experiences highlight the transformative power of cultural festivals, proving that they're not just events to attend but opportunities to connect, learn, and grow.

Volunteer and Thrive

Picture yourself stepping into a local community center, where the hum of activity and laughter fills the air. Volunteering offers a unique blend of personal fulfillment and social connection. It's a chance to meet others who share your values and interests, creating bonds that can enrich your life in unexpected ways. When you give your time and skills to a cause, you not only help others but also find a renewed sense of purpose. The joy of making a tangible difference in your community can be incredibly rewarding, offering a deeper connection to the world around you. Your efforts, no matter how small, contribute to the greater good, leaving a positive mark on society and your heart.

Finding the right volunteer opportunity is an adventure.

Here's my cheat sheet for finding Volunteer Opportunities:

1. **Online Search:** Websites like VolunteerMatch.org and Idealist.org allow you to search for volunteer opportunities based on your location, interests, and skills.

2. **City Website:** The city's official website may have a section dedicated to volunteer opportunities with local government agencies or community programs.

3. **Local Non-profits:** Research into non-profit organizations that align with your interests (e.g., animal shelters, environmental groups, senior centers). Visit their websites or contact them to inquire about volunteer needs.

4. **Community Centers and Libraries:** These places of-

ten have bulletin boards or newsletters listing local volunteer opportunities.

If you're unsure where to begin, volunteer fairs can provide a wealth of information and inspiration. These events bring organizations together, allowing you to explore various roles and find one that resonates with you.

Flexibility is key; choose positions that align with your schedule and passions. Whether it's mentoring young learners, assisting at food banks, or participating in environmental projects, there's a role for every interest and lifestyle. The right match can transform volunteering from a task into a cherished part of your routine.

Long-term volunteering offers the chance to build meaningful relationships. Consistent participation fosters a sense of belonging as you work alongside others toward shared goals. These connections can blossom into friendships, improving your life with companionship and support. To deepen your experience, consider keeping a volunteer journal. Documenting your reflections allows you to track personal growth and insights gained from your service. It's a powerful tool for self-discovery, helping you understand the impact of your contributions and the lessons learned along the way. This practice not only preserves memories but also highlights the positive changes volunteering brings to your life.

Consider the stories of those who have found joy and purpose through volunteering. One retiree, once hesitant about retirement, discovered a passion for teaching literacy to adults. The experience not only reignited her love for education but also introduced her to a community of dedicated volunteers. Another volunteer found fulfillment in helping at an animal shelter, where her compassion for animals fostered friendships and a new sense of belonging, not to mention a never-ending stream of furry kisses. These stories highlight how volunteering can transform lives, offering a path to new relationships and personal fulfillment.

Living and Laughing: Active Adult Communities

Imagine a place where laughter echoes through the hallways, where neighbors greet each other with warmth, and every day offers a new opportunity to connect. Active adult communities are designed to bring people together, creating a vibrant environment where friendships flourish. These communities provide a supportive space for retirees to meet new people, share experiences, and build lasting relationships. Picture a game night, where friendly competition and shared jokes make for an evening of fun. Or a potluck dinner, where each dish tells a story, and conversations flow as freely as the wine. These structured events are more than just activities; they're the heart of a community that thrives on engagement and fellowship.

The shared amenities in active adult communities play a significant role in fostering connections. Gyms, pools, and hobby rooms become social hubs where residents gather, not just to exercise or pursue hobbies but to catch up with friends and meet new people. Imagine starting your day with a swim, exchanging cheerful greetings with fellow swimmers, or joining a fitness class where you sweat and laugh together. These spaces are designed to encourage interaction, providing the perfect backdrop for friendships to form and grow. Whether you're sharing gardening tips in a community plot or enjoying a book club in the library, these shared amenities create countless opportunities to connect with like-minded neighbors.

If you want to dive into your new community, try these tips to get involved:

- **Volunteer:** Offer to help with the planning and execution of events. This is a great way to meet new people and become involved in the community.

- **Attend Events:** Make an effort to attend as many events as possible. This will help you get to know your neighbors and build relationships.

- **Join a Committee:** Consider joining a committee that focuses on an area that interests you, such as social events, fitness, or education.

- **Be Proactive:** Take the initiative and suggest new ideas for events or activities. This will help to keep the community vibrant and engaged.

Welcoming new neighbors is an integral part of building a thriving community. Many active adult communities have welcome committees dedicated to ensuring newcomers feel at home. Consider hosting informal social gatherings, such as coffee mornings or dinner parties, welcoming new residents. These gatherings break the ice and create a warm, inviting atmosphere where friendships can blossom. It's an opportunity to share stories, learn about each other's backgrounds, and discover common interests. By fostering an inclusive environment, you contribute to a community where everyone feels valued and connected.

Engaging in interest-based clubs and groups is another way to build meaningful relationships. Whether you have a passion for gardening, a love for walking, or a knack for crafting, there's likely a club or group that aligns with your interests. Joining these clubs provides a sense of belonging as you connect with others over shared pursuits. Sports leagues, whether it's golf, tennis, or bocce, offer not only the thrill of competition but also the joy of teamwork. These clubs provide structure and routine, enriching your life with activities that keep you engaged and connected.

Consider the inspiring stories of residents who have found lifelong friends and a sense of belonging within active adult communities. One resident, who initially moved in with some hesitation, discovered a love for organizing community events. Her efforts not only brought neighbors together but also led to lasting friendships and a newfound confidence. Another resident found leadership opportunities within the community's walking club, which not only improved his health but also expanded his social circle. These stories highlight the transformative power of active adult communities, proving that these are more than just places to live — they're vibrant, supportive networks where life is enriched by the connections we make. New friends also provide a steady stream of new conversations and stories, which is good for the heart and mind.

Finding Your Tribe: Meetup Groups

Imagine stepping into a room full of people who share your love for gardening, photography, or perhaps even chess. Meetup groups offer this and more, creating spaces where individuals with similar passions can come together and share experiences. These groups are diverse and cater to a wide range of interests—from hobbies and fitness to professional and social gatherings. Whether you're a seasoned hiker looking for trekking buddies or someone keen to learn a new skill, there's likely a Meetup group waiting for you. The beauty of Meetup lies in its ability to bring people together, fostering connections and friendships that might not have formed otherwise. By participating in these groups, you open yourself up to new experiences and the chance to meet people who inspire and motivate you.

Joining Meetup.com is straightforward. It is the largest and most popular platform for finding and joining Meetup groups. Start by creating a profile on their website or mobile app, a process that only takes a few minutes. Once you are set-up, you can search for groups that match your interests and fit your schedule. With the ability to filter by location and activity type, finding the right group becomes a breeze.

Finding the Right Meetup Group:

1. **Define Your Interests:** What are you passionate about? Do you enjoy hiking, cooking, reading, volunteering, or something else? Identify your interests so you can search for relevant groups.

2. **Explore Group Descriptions:** Read through the descriptions of different groups to learn about their focus, activities, and members. Look for groups that align with your interests and have a welcoming atmosphere.

3. **Attend Events:** Once you've found a few groups that interest you, attend some of their events to see if they're a good fit for you. This will allow you to meet the members and assess the group's dynamics.

4. **Ask Questions:** Don't hesitate to ask questions to the group organizers or members to learn more about the group and their activities.

5. **Join Multiple Groups:** Consider joining multiple groups if you have diverse interests or want to expand your social circle.

If, however, you find that your niche interest isn't represented, why not start your own group? Creating a Meetup group allows you to take the lead and gather like-minded individuals, building a community from the ground up. This initiative not only enhances your leadership skills but also positions you as a connector, someone who brings people together over shared passions.

Regular participation is key to maximizing your Meetup experience. Engaging consistently in meetings helps strengthen relationships and ensures that you're an active member of the community. This involvement goes beyond just attending events; it's about contributing to discussions, sharing your knowledge, and supporting others in the group. Consider suggesting collaborative projects or activities that involve all members, fostering a sense of community and teamwork. Whether it's organizing a photography exhibition or a community clean-up, these collaborative efforts create stronger bonds and memories, enhancing the group's dynamic.

Success stories abound in Meetup communities. Take the example of a retiree who joined a local hiking group. Initially a casual participant, she soon became a regular, building friendships with fellow hikers. Through these connections, she discovered new trails and even organized hiking trips, exploring places she'd never imagined. Another senior found a passion for painting through a Meetup art group. What started as a simple interest blossomed into a love for art, leading him to create his own masterpieces and showcase them at local galleries. These stories are just a glimpse of how Meetup can transform your social life, offering opportunities for personal growth, skill development, and lasting friendships.

Wrap-Up: Stronger Together

As you look back on the experiences and connections forged, it's clear that the power of engagement is transformative. Engaging with others not only enriches your retirement but creates a vibrant mural of relationships that add depth and color to your life. Whether through community events, shared hobbies, or spontaneous gatherings, each interaction builds a network of support and joy. The sense of belonging that comes from these connections provides purpose and fulfillment, turning retirement into a chapter of growth and exploration. Embracing these opportunities allows you to blend a rich social landscape, one where laughter, understanding, and companionship is abundant.

Now, it's time to act. Explore at least one of the social opportunities we've discussed. Whether it's joining a local club, volunteering, or participating in a cultural festival, stepping outside your comfort zone can lead to unexpected joy and connection. Consider attending a local event you've never been to or reaching out to a neighbor for a chat over coffee. These small steps can open doors to new friendships and experiences, enriching your life in ways you might not have imagined. Remember, the goal is not just to fill your calendar but to fill your heart with the warmth of genuine connections. By actively participating in your community, you invite a world of possibilities into your life, each one a chance to learn, grow, and connect.

As you move forward, prepare to delve into a world of personal passions and hobbies. This next chapter is all about discovering what lights you up and pursuing it with enthusiasm. Whether it's a long-lost interest or something entirely new, the pursuit of personal passions adds layers of happiness and meaning to your daily life. It allows you to explore your identity beyond titles and roles, focusing on what truly fulfills you. As you embrace these personal pursuits, you'll find that they not only enrich your own life but also enhance the connections you've built, creating a community that supports and uplifts one another.

Retirement is a time of exploration, a chance to redefine what it means to be part of a community. By engaging with others and pursuing your passions, you create a life filled with purpose and joy. The friendships you form and the interests you pursue become the foundation of a fulfilling and vibrant retirement. As you continue this journey, remember that each step you take is an opportunity to connect, grow, and thrive. So go ahead and embrace the adventure with open arms and an open heart. The possibilities are as endless as your imagination, and the impact you make is immeasurable. Take that next step... keep doing!

CHAPTER THREE

Curiosity Never Retires

H ave you ever felt the thrill of figuring out a puzzle or learning something new? It's that spark of excitement when the pieces finally fall into place. This isn't a feeling reserved for youth; it's a lifelong treasure, a gift that keeps giving, no matter the stage of life you're in. Retirement opens a unique window to dive into this world of learning, where the only limits are the ones, you set for yourself. With time on your side, the landscape of education is vast and varied, inviting you to explore topics that have always piqued your curiosity or even those you've never thought of before.

Never Stop Growing ~ Lifelong Learning

Embracing lifelong learning during retirement isn't just about filling the hours; it's about enriching them. Each new skill you acquire or subject you explore adds depth to your days, keeping your mind sharp and engaged. This ongoing pursuit of knowledge feeds your mental agility, which is as important as physical health. It boosts your self-esteem, as mastering new topics or skills can be incredibly satisfying. Moreover, it fosters a sense of purpose, giving your days structure and meaning. Imagine the joy of finally mastering a challenging piano piece or conversing in a new language with newfound confidence. It's these moments that make lifelong learning a rewarding endeavor.

Learning is an adventure that knows no bounds. The beauty of this journey lies in its diversity. You might find yourself drawn to formal education, where you can delve into subjects with academic rigor, or perhaps you're more inclined towards cultural exploration, where learning is as much about experiences as it is about facts. Formal education offers a structured path, guiding you step-by-step through complex topics. It might be a history course that transports you back in time or a science class that unravels the mysteries of the universe. This structured learning environment stimulates the mind, encouraging critical thinking and analysis.

On the other hand, cultural exploration offers a more fluid and experiential approach. It's about immersing yourself in different worlds, whether through art, music, or travel. You may attend a lecture on Renaissance art, followed by a visit to a local gallery where the paintings come to life. Or you'll explore world cuisines, learning about cultures through their culinary traditions. This type of learning isn't confined to textbooks; it's about experiencing life in all its vibrancy. It brings a rich array of experiences that broaden your perspective and deepen your appreciation for the world around you.

Take a moment to reflect on what intrigues you. What subjects have always caught your eye but remained unexplored? Do you have a hobby you're passionate about that could benefit from more in-depth knowledge? Consider jotting down a list of topics or skills you'd like to pursue. Reflect on how these interests align with your values and aspirations. This exercise can help you pinpoint the areas that will bring the most joy and fulfillment, guiding your journey of lifelong learning.

Whether you're uncovering history, exploring global traditions, or appreciating the nuances of art, the path of lifelong learning is uniquely yours. It's a journey that promises not just knowledge but a fuller, more connected life. The world is your classroom, filled with endless possibilities waiting to be discovered. What will you find?

Hands-On Learning: Local Workshops

Imagine the thrill of molding clay into a beautiful vase. Or picture the satisfaction of capturing the perfect photograph, the light and shadows dancing just right. These are the kind of fun, hands-on experiences that local workshops and seminars offer. They invite you to engage directly with instructors and peers, learning through doing rather than just observing. It's the difference between reading a recipe and actually cooking the dish. In these settings, you don't just absorb information; you actively apply it, turning knowledge into skill.

Workshops foster a collaborative environment where feedback flows freely and ideas are exchanged with enthusiasm. Imagine sitting in a painting class, surrounded by others who share your curiosity. As you chat and compare brush strokes, friendships blossom. The social aspect becomes as rewarding as the learning itself. You get the chance to work alongside others, sharing insights and techniques, and in doing so, you often forge connections that extend beyond the workshop. This collaboration not only enhances your learning experience but also enhances your social life, bringing new friends and fresh perspectives into your world.

Where to Get Started:

- **Local Colleges and Universities:** Many institutions offer continuing education or community programs with workshops in various areas, from arts and crafts to technology, personal development, and more. Check their website or contact their continuing education department.

- **Art Clubs and Societies:** If you're interested in visual arts, local art clubs often offer workshops for beginners in painting, drawing, sculpting, or other mediums.

- **Recreation or Community Centers:** These centers frequently host workshops on a variety of topics, catering to different age groups and interests.

- **Libraries:** Libraries are increasingly offering workshops, from computer skills and creative writing to genealogy and local history. Check their event calendar or ask the librarian.

- **Senior Centers:** Many senior centers offer workshops specifically designed for older adults, covering topics like health and wellness, crafts, technology, and more.

- **Chambers of Commerce:** Your local Chamber of Commerce may be aware of local businesses or individuals offering workshops on topics relevant to the community, or they might even host some themselves.

- **Local Businesses:** Some local businesses, like art supply stores, bookstores, culinary shops, or craft stores, may offer workshops related to their products or services.

- **YMCA/YWCA:** These organizations often provide a variety of classes and workshops, including some geared toward seniors.

- **Online Search:** Search for "[your interest] workshops [your city/region]" to see if any individuals or smaller groups are offering specialized instruction in your area. Also, search for "[your interest] classes for seniors [your city/region]."

- **Community Education Programs:** Many communities have dedicated adult and continuing education programs. Search online for "community education [your city/region]."

The key is to look for subjects that ignite your interest, whether it's pottery, painting, or something else entirely.

The beauty of workshops lies in their diversity and flexibility. Each workshop is an opportunity to explore a new facet of yourself, discover hidden talents, and unlock new passions. It's a chance to step outside your comfort zone and see what you're capable of when you give yourself the opportunity to learn. Typically, workshops are only for a limited time. An afternoon or evening to learn and try. It's a significant first step before signing up for an entire class on a topic.

A few years ago, I attended a Backyard Beekeeping workshop out of sheer curiosity. I never imagined that I would have a hive of my own. In the workshop, I got to harvest honey from frame to jar and go home with a bottle of the sweet stuff. That simple afternoon workshop started a brand-new hobby that has yielded pounds of my own honey and a garden that is healthier than ever due to its new pollinating neighbors. It could have gone the other way, where I had a fun afternoon trying something totally new and nothing more. Either way, this simple workshop was a win in my book. Hands-on learning can transform retirement, turning it into a time of discovery and connection.

Rediscover the Classroom: Local College Courses

Imagine walking into a classroom filled with eager minds, a space buzzing with the promise of discovery. This might seem familiar, perhaps a scene from the past, but now, as a retiree, you're returning with a fresh perspective and boundless curiosity. Local community colleges are a treasure trove of courses waiting to be explored, covering a broad spectrum of topics.

The beauty of these programs lies in their flexibility. Evening and weekend classes cater to your schedule, allowing you to pursue learning without disrupting your newfound freedom. This flexibility means you can engage with subjects at your own pace, making education a part of your life without overwhelming it.

Enrolling in a community college course is a straightforward process designed to be as welcoming as the classrooms themselves. Start by exploring the course catalog online or in person. Once you find a course that piques your interest, the next step is the application process. This can often be completed online, or you can visit the college in person for a more hands-on approach. Meeting with an academic advisor is a valuable step, offering guidance tailored to your interests and helping you navigate the choices available. Advisors are there to assist, ensuring you find the right fit and feel confident in your decision. This support makes the transition back into education smooth and rewarding.

Most Popular Programs and Courses for Retirees:

- **Lifelong Learning Programs:** These non-credit programs are specifically designed for older adults and cover a wide range of topics, from history and literature to art and music. They often emphasize social interaction and intellectual stimulation.

- **Computer Skills and Technology:** Many retirees want to improve their computer skills for communication and entertainment or even to start a new hobby like digital photography or blogging. Community colleges offer courses for all levels, from basic computer literacy to more advanced software programs.

- **Arts and Humanities:** Courses in painting, drawing, creative writing, music appreciation, and history are popular among retirees who want to explore their creative side or delve deeper into subjects they've always been interested in.

- **Health and Wellness:** Staying healthy and active is a priority for many retirees. Community colleges offer courses in fitness, nutrition, stress management, and other health-related topics and are great places to find exercise buddies.

- **Languages:** Learning a new language can be a rewarding experience for retirees, whether for travel, cultural enrichment, or simply a mental challenge.

- **Personal Enrichment:** Courses in areas like gardening, cooking, financial planning, and home improvement are also popular among retirees who want to enhance their personal lives.

Pro Tip:

- **Audit Options:** Some community colleges allow seniors to audit courses for a reduced fee or even for free, providing an excellent opportunity to learn without the pressure of grades or exams.

The benefits of classroom learning extend far beyond the subjects themselves. In-person classes are excellent environments for social and intellectual engagement, fostering real-time discussions and collaboration. These interactions stimulate the mind, encouraging you to think critically and engage with diverse perspectives. The classroom becomes a hub of networking, where connections are formed over shared interests and lively debates. Community colleges also offer extensive resources to support your learning journey, from well-stocked libraries to study groups that provide collaborative learning experiences. These resources enrich the educational experience, offering tools and spaces that enhance understanding and expand your skills and knowledge.

Consider the story of a retiree who decided to learn a new language, a dream long deferred. Enrolling in a local college course, she found herself immersed in not only the language but the culture it represented. Each class was a window into a new world, filled with cultural insights and connections that transcended mere vocabulary. The experience was transformative, reigniting a passion for learning and opening doors to new friendships and adventures. This story is a testament to the power of education in retirement, illustrating how returning to the classroom can be a catalyst for personal growth and fulfillment.

As you consider this path, remember that the classroom is not just a place of learning; it's a space where you can explore new identities and passions. The opportunity to engage with new subjects and interact with others who share your curiosity is invaluable. It's more than acquiring knowledge; it's about enriching your life with experiences that challenge and delight. The classroom is your gateway to a more connected world, where every lesson learned is a step toward greater understanding and joy.

Click, Learn, Grow: Online Classes

The world of online learning is like an open library, its doors wide and welcoming, inviting you to explore an endless array of subjects from the comfort of your home. One of the most significant advantages of platforms like Coursera, Udemy, and edX is their flexibility. These platforms allow you to learn at your own pace, whether you're a night owl or an early bird. You can dive into a course on digital photography at midnight or explore a new language over your morning coffee. The constraints of a traditional classroom disappear, giving you the freedom to tailor your learning experience to fit your lifestyle. This flexibility means you can balance learning with other activities, whether it's caring for grandchildren or tending to a garden. The beauty of these platforms lies in their accessibility, allowing you to transform any space into your personal classroom, where learning can happen anytime, anywhere.

The variety of subjects available online is staggering. You can delve into technology and learn to code or explore personal development courses that help you cultivate mindfulness and resilience. Creative skills like painting or writing are just a click away, opening doors to new hobbies and passions. Each course is a gateway to new knowledge, offering a structured path to explore areas that intrigue you. The choices are vast, ensuring there's something for everyone, no matter what your interests. This range of topics means you can always find something that resonates with your curiosity, ensuring that boredom is never an option. Online learning becomes a personal journey, one where you can continually discover and grow.

Choosing the right online course requires a bit of research. It's essential to evaluate the quality of the course, ensuring it meets your expectations and educational needs. Start by reading reviews from past students, which can offer valuable insight into the course's strengths and weaknesses. Checking the credentials of the instructor is also crucial; an experienced and knowledgeable teacher can make all the difference. Many platforms allow you to preview content before committing, giving you a taste of what to expect. This sneak peek can help you decide if the course aligns with your interests and learning style, making the selection process more informed. Remember, the goal is to find a course that not only interests you but also challenges and inspires you.

<u>Comparing Online Learning Platforms (ordered in my preference for retirees):</u>

The platform you choose depends on your learning style, budget, and the specific skill you want to acquire. Here's a general comparison:

1. **Udemy:** Huge marketplace with a vast range of courses, often at discounted prices. Quality can vary, so read reviews carefully.

2. **Skillshare:** Emphasis on creative skills, with project-based learning and a subscription model.

3. **MasterClass:** This series features celebrity instructors in various fields. It offers high-quality production value but a higher price point.

4. **Academic Earth:** A curated collection of free online courses from universities.

5. **Open Yale Courses:** Free access to lectures and course materials from Yale University.

6. **MIT OpenCourseware:** Free educational materials from MIT courses.

7. **LinkedIn Learning (formerly Lynda.com):** Good for business, creative, and tech skills, integrated with the LinkedIn platform.

8. **Khan Academy:** Free platform with a focus on K-12 education but also has some college-level and skill-based content.

9. **CreativeLive:** Live and on-demand workshops for creatives.

10. **Domestika:** Courses focused on creative skills taught by professionals.

11. **Coursera:** Offers courses, Specializations, and even degrees from top universities worldwide. Strong in various fields, often with financial aid options.

12. **edX:** Similar to Coursera, partnering with universities globally. Known for STEM courses and micro-credentials.

Online learning also offers a social dimension, connecting you with others who share your interests. Discussion boards and forums provide a space for learners to engage in conversations, exchange ideas, and offer support. These virtual communities can be a source of motivation, offering encouragement and camaraderie as you progress through the course. Participating in virtual study groups allows you to collaborate with other students, enhancing your understanding and making learning a collaborative effort. This engagement enriches the learning experience, transforming it from a solitary endeavor into a social one. It's about connecting, sharing, and growing together, even if you're miles apart.

For some, the technical aspects of online learning can be a hurdle. Ensuring reliable internet access is a must, as is familiarizing yourself with the platform's navigation. But don't let these challenges deter you. Many platforms offer tutorials and support to help you get started, making the transition smoother. Taking the time to understand the tools at your disposal can help you feel more confident and ready to embrace online learning. It's about creating a comfortable space where you can focus on learning, free from distractions. With the proper setup, online education becomes an engaging and rewarding experience.

Overcoming Technical Difficulties:

Sadly, tech issues are part of the online learning experience. Here's how to tackle them:

- **Test Your Equipment:** Before starting a course,

check your internet connection, microphone, speakers/headphones, and webcam (if needed).

- **Browser Compatibility:** Ensure your browser is up-to-date and compatible with the learning platform.

- **Clear Cache and Cookies:** This often resolves minor glitches.

- **Restart Everything:** The classic IT solution! Restart your computer, router, and modem.

- **Check Platform Status:** See if the learning platform itself is experiencing outages or technical issues.

- **Search the Help Center:** Most platforms have extensive FAQs and troubleshooting guides.

- **Contact Support:** If you can't find a solution, don't hesitate to contact the platform's technical support.

- **Have a Backup Plan:** Have a secondary device or internet connection (like using a hotspot through your mobile device) available in case of emergencies.

- **Patience is Key:** Remember that technical difficulties happen. Take a deep breath, troubleshoot systematically, and don't get discouraged.

Staying motivated in an online course is key to success. Setting personal goals can provide direction and keep you on track. Whether it's completing a lesson each week or dedicating a specific time each day to study, these goals create a sense of accountability. Joining online learning communities can also boost motivation. These groups offer support and encouragement, helping you stay engaged and committed. With these strategies, you can navigate the world of online learning with confidence, embracing its opportunities and challenges with enthusiasm.

History on Your Doorstep

Imagine strolling through the quiet, hallowed halls of your local museum, the echoes of the past whispering through its corridors. Each exhibit offers a window into a world gone by, a chance to connect with the stories and struggles of those who walked the earth before us. Local museums are treasure troves of regional history and culture, showcasing artifacts and narratives that have shaped your community's identity. These spaces invite you to delve into the heart of your town, exploring the tapestry of events and characters that have contributed to its unique flavor. Engaging with these stories not only satisfy a curiosity about the past but also deepens your connection to the place you call home.

Beyond the museum walls, public archives hold a wealth of untapped knowledge waiting to be discovered. Local libraries and historical societies house documents and records that bring history to life. Whether it's the minutes of a town meeting from a century ago or a collection of old photographs, these archives provide a tangible link to history. Accessing these resources can reveal surprising connections to your own life, perhaps unearthing family ties or revealing the origins of local traditions. As you navigate these archives, you become both detective and storyteller, piecing together the lives and events that have shaped your world.

Here are some of my favorite sections to check out in your local archives:

This is also a great activity to do with the grandkids. Make it a treasure hunt where they must find one cool thing about your city, neighborhood, or home.

- **Personal documents** - Letters, diaries, family Bibles, photographs, and scrapbooks detailing personal lives and experiences

- **Government records** - Census data, property deeds,

marriage and birth certificates, court records, and local government documents providing information about individuals and their families (what happened in your house or on your land before you lived there)

- **Newspaper clippings** - Articles about local events, people, and businesses. It's fun to see what the big news was on the day you were born or what happened 100 (or 1000) years ago.

- **Maps and plats** - Historical maps showing property boundaries and development changes over time.

- **Business records** - Company documents, ledgers, and correspondence providing insight into local economic history. Learn more about the employers of your parents or grandparents.

- **Oral histories** - Audio recordings of interviews with long-time residents sharing personal stories and perspectives.

Many museums, archives (and even libraries) offer guided tours, which is a great way to fast-track your historical exploration. These tours, led by knowledgeable guides, offer in-depth insights that bring exhibits to life, providing context and depth to what you see. Who knows? You might be so inspired that you become one of those docents in the future.

Understanding history isn't just about looking backward; it's about finding inspiration for the present and future. By connecting with your cultural heritage, you gain a deeper appreciation for your roots and the community that surrounds you. History has a way of illuminating the path forward, offering lessons in resilience, innovation, and community. It encourages ongoing learning and exploration, stimulating intellectual curiosity and broadening your perspective on current events and trends. The past is an influential teacher, providing context and clarity as you navigate your own life's journey.

My husband got me on the ancestry bandwagon. He found out one of his relatives was a pallbearer for Abraham Lincoln, and that was it. I wanted to know what my ancestors did. I ended up organizing a family trip to retrace our ancestor's roots. It was a trip of a lifetime filled with laughter, tears, and tons of new memories. In the end, I had so many documents and materials that I didn't know what to do with them.

Here's my list of what to do to preserve and share your family history:

- **Digitize Everything:** Scan photos, documents, and other memorabilia to create digital copies. This protects the originals and makes them easy to share.

- **Organize Your Files:** Create a clear and logical system for organizing your digital and physical files.

- **Create a Family Website or Blog:** Share your research and family stories online.

- **Write a Family History Book:** Compile your research, photos, and stories into a book for your family.

- **Share at Family Gatherings:** Bring photos and stories to family reunions or gatherings.

- **Use Archival Quality Materials:** When storing physical documents and photos, use acid-free paper, archival sleeves, and appropriate storage containers.

- **Back-Up Your Data:** Regularly back up your digital files to prevent data loss.

Such discoveries often bring a profound sense of pride and connection, bridging the gap between past and present. For some, these findings spark a newfound interest in historical reenactments, where they can step into the shoes of their ancestors and bring history to life. Participating in reenactments or tours provides an immersive experience, offering insight into the daily lives and challenges faced by those who came before us. These activities allow you to engage with history tangibly, fostering a deeper understanding and appreciation for the past.

Through these explorations, you not only uncover personal histories but also contribute to preserving the stories and lessons of history for future generations. Each discovery adds a new layer of understanding, enriching your life with knowledge and connection. Whether through joining a society, attending workshops, or participating in reenactments, the journey of history and ancestry exploration is as rewarding as it is enlightening. What is your story?

Speak Your Mind: New Languages

Imagine the thrill of ordering a meal in a quaint café in Paris or striking up a conversation in Spanish on the streets of Buenos Aires. Learning a new language opens doors to not just words and phrases but to entire cultures and societies. It enriches your life with new experiences and opportunities, making the world a more inviting and accessible place. Beyond the adventure, there's a profound cognitive benefit to embracing a new tongue. Studies show that language learning can enhance cognitive function and memory, acting as a mental workout that keeps the brain agile. It's not just about learning to speak; it's about keeping the mind active and engaged.

Cognitive Benefits (sign me up for these):

- **Improved Memory:** Learning vocabulary and grammar strengthens memory skills.

- **Enhanced Problem-Solving:** Navigating different language structures and meanings improves problem-solving abilities.

- **Increased Multitasking Skills:** Switching between languages enhances multitasking capabilities.

- **Better Attention and Focus:** The mental effort required for language learning improves concentration.

- **Enhanced Cognitive Flexibility:** Being able to think in different linguistic frameworks increases cognitive flexibility.

- **Improved Decision-Making:** Studies suggest bilinguals make more rational decisions.

- **Increased Empathy:** Learning about other cultures through language can foster empathy and understanding.

- **Delayed Cognitive Decline:** Some research indicates that bilingualism may delay the onset of age-related cognitive decline, including dementia.

The social benefits of learning a language are equally appealing. Knowing another language can transform your travel experiences, opening a whole new local experience and navigating new environments with ease. Imagine the joy of understanding the nuances of a conversation in a bustling market or the satisfaction of reading a novel in its original language. These skills open cultural experiences that enrich your life, from watching foreign films with an understanding of their dialogue to participating in cultural events that require at least a basic grasp of the language. Moreover, speaking another language can lead to new friendships, connecting you with people from different backgrounds who share your passion for languages. It's a bridge to new worlds, both abroad and at home.

Fortunately, there are numerous resources available to help you embark on this linguistic adventure. Apps and platforms like Duolingo, Rosetta Stone, and Babbel offer flexible, self-paced learning that fits into your schedule. These new language learning tools are designed to make it fun, using games and challenges to reinforce vocabulary and grammar. They allow you to learn wherever you are, whether it's during your morning coffee or while waiting for an appointment. If you prefer a more personal approach, consider joining a community language exchange. These groups, available both locally and online, provide the chance to practice speaking with native speakers and fellow learners. They offer a safe and supportive space where you can hone your skills and receive feedback, making the learning process dynamic and social.

Integrating a new language into your daily life can be both practical and enjoyable. Another option is to watch foreign films or read books in the language you're learning, which is a fun way to get more context and immersion, helping you grasp idioms and cultural references. Listening to music or podcasts in your chosen language can also enhance your understanding and pronunciation. The key is to make language practice a regular part of your routine, weaving it into your daily activities so that it becomes a natural part of your life. This consistent exposure helps to solidify your learning, making the new language feel more familiar and intuitive.

Setting realistic goals is crucial in language learning. Start by identifying milestones that are achievable yet challenging. Perhaps your first goal is to complete a beginner-level course, followed by having a simple conversation with a language partner once a week. These milestones provide direction and motivation, helping you track your progress and celebrate your achievements. Remember, language learning is a gradual process, so be patient and persistent. Each step forward, no matter how small, brings you closer to fluency and the rewards that come with it. Carpe Diem!

Wrap-Up: Learning Without Limits

Picture your mind as a vast landscape dotted with uncharted territories waiting for exploration. Retirement offers a golden opportunity to navigate these areas, each new experience sparking excitement and fulfillment. Learning is not bound by age; it's a dynamic process that molds and refines you, keeping your cognitive faculties sharp and vibrant. Imagine the thrill of acquiring a new skill or delving into a subject that piqued your curiosity long ago. It's about rekindling that spark of curiosity, igniting a fire that enriches your life with knowledge and satisfaction. This chapter serves as a reminder that retirement isn't a retreat from life but an invitation to push boundaries and explore the endless possibilities that learning offers.

Taking the first step in this ongoing adventure is both empowering and exhilarating. Consider enrolling in a course at a local college or exploring the myriad online learning options available. These platforms open doors to subjects you may have never imagined. Or you're drawn to the idea of attending a local workshop or seminar, where hands-on experiences and direct interaction provide a tactile connection to learning. These experiences not only broaden your horizon but also introduce you to new people, enhancing your social network with individuals who share your enthusiasm for growth. Each course and each workshop are a stepping-stone on the path of lifelong learning, a journey that is both personal and communal.

Engaging with history and culture offers a variety of learning experiences. By joining a historical society or participating in cultural studies, you connect with the past in meaningful ways. These activities allow you to see the world through different lenses, deepening your understanding of diverse traditions and histories. Such engagement fosters empathy and appreciation, enriching your perspective and broadening your worldview. It's about more than just facts and dates;

it's about connecting with the stories that shape our world and finding your place within that narrative. Through these explorations, you gain not just knowledge but a deeper connection to the world around you.

Now, as you stand on the threshold of these opportunities, embrace the adventure of lifelong learning with open arms. Let it be a source of joy and fulfillment, a way to stay mentally agile and engaged. Learning is not a race; there's no finish line to cross. Instead, see it as a continuous process, an ever-evolving landscape where each new experience adds depth and color to your life. Take that first step, whether it's enrolling in a course, attending a seminar, or joining a club. These actions are not just about gaining knowledge but about creating a life rich with experiences and connections.

As you move forward, remember that every new skill acquired, and every piece of knowledge gained contributes to a life of purpose and joy. Retirement is a time for growth, exploration, and the creation of new opportunities for personal and intellectual development. So, keep your curiosity alive and your mind open. The world is vast, and there's always something new to discover. With this mindset, the possibilities are truly limitless.

Now, let your curiosity guide you into the next chapter of your life. We'll explore how to nurture your physical health and vitality, ensuring you have the energy and strength to embrace these new adventures.

"The best way to find yourself is to lose yourself in the service of others." ~ Mahatma Gandhi

Unlock the Power of Generosity

Would you help someone you've never met, even if you never got any recognition for it?

Here's where you come in. You've probably heard the saying, "People judge a book by its cover (and its reviews)." It's true. So, I'm asking for a small favor on behalf of a retiree who could truly benefit from this book. Please help that retiree by leaving a review.

It costs you nothing and takes less than 60 seconds to make a huge difference. Want to feel good knowing you've made a real impact? Simply scan the QR code and share your thoughts.

Thank you from the bottom of my heart. Let's get back to helping you thrive in your next chapter!

SCAN ME

CHAPTER FOUR

Globetrotter's Guide

The world is vast and full of wonders, just waiting to be discovered at your own pace. Imagine the freedom to wake up in a new place, the anticipation of exploring a town you've never visited, or the thrill of learning about a culture entirely different from your own. Retirement offers the perfect opportunity to turn these dreams into reality. It's a time when your schedule is your own, and the world is your playground. You might have spent years planning for this moment, and now that it's here, the possibilities are truly endless.

The World Awaits

Traveling isn't just about moving from one place to another; it's about the experiences you gather along the way. Whether it's a short drive to a nearby town or a longer journey across the seas, each trip offers a chance to see the world through fresh eyes. Imagine the joy of stumbling upon a quaint café hidden down a cobblestone alley or the delight of tasting a dish whose flavors dance on your tongue, each bite a new discovery. When you travel, you're not just a visitor; you're an explorer, uncovering the stories and secrets that each destination holds.

In retirement, travel can break the monotony of daily life, offering a welcome change of scenery and pace. It allows you to step out of your comfort zone and into a world of adventure. Each trip, whether near or far, can invigorate your spirit and open your mind to new possibilities. It's a form of self-care that nurtures the soul, reminding you that life is full of wonders waiting to be explored. Plus, the memories you make on these journeys can be cherished for a lifetime, adding richness and depth to your personal story.

Nurturing your inner explorer doesn't always require a passport; sometimes, it means rediscovering the beauty in your own backyard. There may be a nearby nature reserve you've always wanted to visit or a local festival that celebrates the unique culture of your town. These local excursions offer the chance to connect with your community and appreciate the intricacies of the world around you. They provide a sense of adventure without the need for extensive planning or travel, making them perfect for those spontaneous days when you're eager to explore but prefer to stay closer to home.

For those with a penchant for more distant adventures, the world is truly your oyster. Consider the immersive learning adventures offered by travel companies like Road Scholar, which cater specifically to seniors. These tours are designed to provide stress-free travel experiences with planned logistics and expert guides. Imagine exploring the Scottish Highlands, where every hill and loch tells tales of history and legend, or embarking on a yacht voyage along the Croatian coastline, where each port introduces you to the vibrant cultures of the Mediterranean.

Retirement opens a world of travel possibilities! Here are some of my favorite travel destinations for retirees. I've kept in mind factors like accessibility, pace, interests, and budget:

For Relaxing & Cultural Immersion:

- **River Cruises (Europe):** A fantastic way to see multiple cities without the hassle of packing and unpacking. The pace is generally relaxed, and you can explore different cultures along the Rhine, Danube, or Douro rivers.

- **Tuscany, Italy:** Charming countryside with rolling hills, vineyards, delicious food, and art. Rent a villa or stay in a small town for a slower pace of life.

- **Provence, France:** Like Tuscany, Provence offers beautiful landscapes, charming villages, and a rich cultural heritage. It is perfect for foodies and art lovers.

- **Costa Rica:** This country has beautiful beaches, lush rainforests, and abundant wildlife. It offers a mix of adventure and relaxation, with many eco-lodges and resorts catering to a more mature clientele.

- **Hawaii (Big Island or Kauai):** These islands offer stunning scenery, beautiful beaches, and a relaxed atmosphere. They also offer a variety of activities, from hiking and snorkeling to simply relaxing by the pool.

For History Buffs:

- **Kyoto, Japan:** Ancient temples, beautiful gardens, and traditional tea ceremonies. A fascinating glimpse into Japanese culture and history.

- **Athens, Greece:** The cradle of Western civilization, with iconic landmarks like the Acropolis and

Parthenon.

- **Rome, Italy:** A city steeped in history, with ancient ruins, Renaissance art, and the Vatican City.

- **Egypt (Nile River Cruise):** Explore ancient temples, pyramids, and tombs along the Nile River.

- **Peru (Machu Picchu & Sacred Valley):** Discover the mysteries of the Inca civilization in the Andes Mountains.

For Adventure Seekers (at a comfortable pace):

- **National Parks of the USA (Grand Canyon, Yellowstone, Yosemite):** Stunning natural beauty and opportunities for hiking, wildlife viewing, and photography. Choose trails and activities appropriate for your fitness level.

- **Galapagos Islands:** Unique wildlife and incredible scenery. Cruises are a popular way to explore the islands.

- **New Zealand:** Breathtaking landscapes, from mountains and glaciers to beaches and fjords. Offers a range of activities, from hiking and kayaking to wine tasting.

- **Iceland:** Dramatic landscapes with glaciers, volcanoes, waterfalls, and hot springs. Offers a unique travel experience.

For Budget-Friendly Travel:

- **Southeast Asia (Thailand, Vietnam, Cambodia):** Affordable travel destination with beautiful beaches, delicious food, and rich culture.

- **Portugal:** Offers a similar experience to Spain but at

a lower cost. Beautiful cities like Lisbon and Porto, as well as the Algarve region for beaches.

- **Mexico (various locations):** From the beaches of Cancun and Riviera Maya to the colonial cities of Oaxaca and San Miguel de Allende, Mexico offers a variety of options for different interests and budgets.

As you consider your travel options, remember that exploration is as much about the journey as the destination. The people you meet and the stories you share along the way enrich the experience, turning it into something more than just a trip. Joining travel clubs can offer the company of fellow adventurers, each bringing their perspectives and stories to the mix. These groups often organize themed tours, like wildlife safaris or historical journeys, providing unique opportunities to explore both domestic and international destinations. Whether you're sipping wine in France or tracing ancient paths in Greece, travel clubs make the world feel more connected and accessible.

Travel's true beauty lies in its ability to keep curiosity alive, even as the years go by. It reminds us that there's always more to see, learn, and experience. So, whether you're wandering the charming streets of a nearby town or exploring the far reaches of the globe, each journey adds a new chapter to your story, one filled with wonder, excitement, and discovery.

Short Escapes, Big Adventures

Imagine waking up on a Saturday morning with the freedom to decide where the day will take you. There's a certain magic in the spontaneity of short escapes, where the only thing on your agenda is fun. Day trips and weekend getaways offer a delightful break from routine without the need for elaborate planning or packing. They provide the perfect chance to explore nearby gems and support local businesses while saving on the hassle of extended travel. Whether it's a leisurely drive to a neighboring town or a quick train ride to a nearby city, these short journeys can be both refreshing and invigorating. They allow you to escape the everyday and immerse yourself in new surroundings, all within a day's reach.

The joy of these short getaways lies in their simplicity. You can leave the heavy luggage at home and instead focus on the experience. Imagine spending a sunny afternoon wandering through the showy displays of a botanical garden or arboretum, where every turn reveals a new palette of colors and fragrances. These serene settings offer a peaceful retreat, allowing you to connect with nature and enjoy the tranquility of your surroundings. Perhaps you're drawn to the arts, so a visit to a local gallery or festival might be the thing. The creative energy and cultural immersion found in these venues can be both inspiring and uplifting, sparking new ideas and conversations.

Nature reserves and parks present another enticing option, offering opportunities for scenic walks and picnics that nourish both body and soul. The gentle rustle of leaves, the chirping of birds, and the aroma of the earth after a light rain—all these sensory delights await you in these natural havens. A well-planned day trip can rejuvenate your spirit and provide a much-needed escape from the hustle and bustle of daily life. To make the most of these outings, check local event calendars for unique happenings that align with your interests. Whether it's a food festival, outdoor concert, or farmers' market, these events add a layer of excitement and discovery to your journey.

Here are some ideas to get you going:

Day Trips (within a couple of hours' drive):

- **Beaches:** Even if you live near the coast, exploring different beaches can be refreshing. Look for beaches with accessible walkways, benches, and restroom facilities. Consider packing a picnic to enjoy the ocean views.

- **Nature Trails & Parks:** Many areas have beautiful nature trails and parks. Choose trails with paved or well-maintained surfaces for easier walking. Check for parks with accessible amenities and consider bringing a walking stick for added stability.

- **Botanical Gardens:** These offer beautiful scenery and often have paved paths and benches for resting. Many botanical gardens also have accessible restrooms and other facilities.

- **Local Museums & Historical Sites:** Explore the history and culture of your region by visiting local museums and historical sites. Check for accessibility features beforehand.

- **Art Galleries & Studios:** If you're interested in art, visit local galleries and studios. Many offer demonstrations or workshops.

- **Wineries or Breweries (with transportation):** Enjoy a relaxing day of wine or beer tasting. Hire a driver or use a ride-sharing service to ensure safe transit.

- **Small Towns & Quaint Villages:** Explore charming small towns with unique shops, restaurants, and historical architecture. Many offer a slower pace of life and a chance to connect with local culture.

Weekend Getaways (a bit further afield):

- **Nearby Cities:** Explore larger cities within driving distance. Look for attractions that cater to your interests, such as museums, theaters, or historical sites. Consider staying in a hotel with accessible amenities.

- **State Parks & Lodges:** Many state parks offer comfortable lodging options and access to natural beauty.

Look for parks with accessible trails and facilities.

• **Resorts with Senior-Friendly Amenities:** Some resorts cater specifically to seniors, offering accessible accommodations, activities, and dining options.

• **Casinos (if interested):** Some casinos offer shows, restaurants, and other entertainment options in addition to gaming. Consider transportation options and accessibility features.

Planning a successful day trip involves a few simple steps to ensure a smooth and enjoyable experience. Start by selecting a destination that piques your interest, and if it's a popular spot, consider booking accommodations or tickets in advance to avoid any last-minute hiccups. Packing a small essentials kit with sunscreen, water, snacks, and comfortable clothing will keep you prepared for whatever the day brings. Accessibility is also important, so choose places that cater to all mobility levels, ensuring that everyone can join in the fun.

Creating sample itineraries can add structure to your day while leaving room for spontaneous adventures. Picture an "Art and Culture Tour," starting with a visit to a local gallery, followed by a historical walking tour through charming streets. Or perhaps a "Nature and Relaxation Day," beginning with a morning hike in a state park and concluding with an afternoon at a nearby botanical garden. These curated experiences allow you to savor the best of what each destination has to offer, creating memories that linger long after the day has ended.

To enhance the experience and create lasting memories, consider organizing group day trips with friends or family. Sharing these adventures with loved ones not only strengthens bonds but also enriches the journey with shared laughter and storytelling. Whether it's a picnic by the lake, a stroll through an art exhibition, or a scenic drive through the countryside, these collective experiences become cherished moments that bring joy and connection. The beauty of short escapes lies in their ability to bring people together, reminding us that sometimes the most memorable adventures are found close to home.

Uncovering Local Treasures

You might be surprised to learn that hidden gems of history lie just around the corner, waiting to be discovered and explored. Visiting local historical landmarks and museums offers more than just a peek into the past; it increases your understanding of the community and its roots. Each artifact, plaque, and portrait tells a story of the people and events that have shaped the area you call home. Imagine wandering through a museum, the air thick with the scent of aged wood and dust, as you trace your fingers over the glass housing a century-old document or peer closely at a faded photograph. Every detail carries a whisper of days gone by, instantly transporting you to the past.

Participating in guided tours is another way to delve deeper. These tours often highlight lesser-known facts and anecdotes, bringing the past to life with vivid storytelling and insightful perspectives. A tour guide might lead you down cobblestone streets, pointing out architectural features or hidden alleyways that once witnessed momentous events, enhancing your experience with tales of triumph and tragedy that textbooks often overlook.

Exploring local history is not just about what you see but also about what you discover. Hidden gems lie in the most unexpected places, waiting to be found by the curious and the persistent. Historical societies are invaluable resources for those eager to delve into the local past. These organizations often house archives brimming with documents, photographs, and personal letters that reveal intimate details of the community's evolution. By reaching out to these societies, you gain access to a wealth of information about historical sites, landmarks, and events that have shaped the area. You may find yourself piecing together the puzzle of your town's history, one artifact at a time. And don't forget about the historical markers and plaques scattered throughout neighborhoods and cities. These often-overlooked signs provide clues to significant occurrences and figures, guiding you on a self-directed exploration of history's footprint in your town.

Here are some other thought starters to find local historical landmarks and museums:

- **Local Historical Society Museum:** This is often the best starting point for local history. They'll have exhibits and information specific to the town or region.

- **Regional or County Historical Society Museums:** These museums cover a wider area and may have collections related to specific themes (e.g., maritime history, agricultural history).

- **State or Provincial Museums:** These more prominent museums offer a broader perspective on the history of your state or province.

- **Specialized Museums:** Look for museums dedicated to specific topics, such as transportation (trains, planes, automobiles), industry (mining, textiles), or specific cultural groups.

- **Historic Homes and Sites:** Many communities have preserved historic homes or other buildings that offer a glimpse into the past.

- **National Parks and Monuments:** These often have historical significance in addition to their natural beauty. Check for visitor centers or interpretive programs that discuss the area's history.

- **Local Cemeteries:** Old cemeteries can be a valuable resource for genealogical research and regional history. Look for interesting headstones or research the families buried there.

- **Architectural Walking Tours:** Explore your town or city on foot, looking for older buildings and researching their history and architectural styles.

- **Monuments and Memorials:** These public spaces often commemorate significant historical events or figures.

- **Battlefields and Historic Trails:** If your area has a history of conflict or significant migration, explore battlefields or historic trails.

Documenting your historical explorations can add another layer to the experience. Consider creating a scrapbook or blog to capture the spirit of your discoveries. Collect photos, ticket stubs, and brochures from each site you visit, arranging them in a way that tells a story. Add your thoughts and reflections in a journal entry, noting what surprised you or struck a chord. This personal documentation serves as both a keepsake and a way to share your journey with others. Storytelling is a powerful tool for keeping history alive, and by sharing your experiences, you encourage others to embark on their own historical explorations. Whether it's recounting a fascinating fact to a friend or writing a blog post that reaches a broader audience, your stories breathe life into the past, ensuring that the echoes of history continue to resonate in the present.

Imagine the thrill of discovering a personal connection to local history through genealogy research. Perhaps a visit to a nearby museum reveals that your great-grandparents were part of a significant local movement, or an old photograph in the archives bears a striking resemblance to a relative. These connections transform historical exploration from an abstract study into a profoundly personal experience, bridging the gap between past and present. Consider the story of a retiree who, through genealogy research, unearthed a family tie to a historic event in their hometown. This discovery sparked a passion for local history, leading to further study and involvement in community heritage projects. Or think of the community member who revitalized interest in local history by organizing educational tours and sharing their findings with neighbors and visitors alike. By bringing history to life, they fostered a sense of pride and connection within the community, reminding all the shared stories that unite them.

Wander Far, Wander Wide: Travel Clubs

Imagine the thrill of setting off on a new adventure but with the added comfort of a group of like-minded explorers by your side. Travel clubs offer this and more, transforming solo travel into a shared experience rich with camaraderie and discovery. One of the most significant advantages of joining a travel club is the ease it brings to planning. With logistics handled by experienced coordinators, you can focus on the excitement of the journey rather than the nitty-gritty details. This means more time for you to savor the joy of travel and less time spent navigating itineraries or booking accommodations. Additionally, travel clubs often have access to exclusive deals and discounts, making it easier on your wallet to explore destinations that might otherwise seem out of reach. The shared adventures within a group setting also mean that every new experience is peppered with laughter and stories, turning strangers into friends as you explore together.

Travel clubs cater to a wide array of interests, offering themed tours that dive deep into specific passions. Perhaps you've always dreamed of embarking on a wine-tasting journey through the rolling vineyards of Tuscany, where each sip tells a tale of the land and its people. Or a wildlife safari in

Africa, where the thrill of spotting majestic creatures in their natural habitat leaves you breathless, is more your style. Historical journeys hold their own allure, allowing you to walk in the footsteps of those who came before, uncovering the rich tapestry of human history. Whether your heart yearns for the charm of domestic destinations or the allure of international landscapes, travel clubs provide the perfect avenue to explore both locally and globally, satisfying every wanderlust craving.

Specific Travel Clubs Catering to Different Interests:

Travel clubs are as diverse as travel itself! Here are some examples:

- **Adventure Travel Clubs:** For active seniors who enjoy hiking, trekking, kayaking, and other outdoor activities. Some specialize in specific types of adventures, like wildlife viewing or exploring remote areas.

- **Cultural & Educational Travel Clubs:** Focus on enriching experiences like museum visits, historical tours, language learning, and interactions with local cultures. Often feature expert guides or lecturers.

- **Food & Wine Travel Clubs:** Cater to culinary enthusiasts with trips that include cooking classes, wine tastings, visits to local markets, and dining at top restaurants.

- **Luxury Travel Clubs:** Offer high-end accommodation, exclusive experiences, and personalized service. Trips often include private tours, gourmet meals, and stays at five-star hotels.

- **Singles Travel Clubs:** Designed for solo travelers who want to explore the world with a group of like-minded individuals. It can be a great way to meet new people and avoid single supplement charges.

- **Special Interest Travel Clubs:** Cater to specific hobbies or passions, like photography, bird watching, gardening, or genealogy.

- **Senior Travel Clubs:** Some clubs specialize in travel for seniors, offering itineraries and activities that are tailored to their needs and interests. Accessibility is often a key consideration.

- **Alumni Travel Clubs:** Many universities and colleges have alums travel programs that offer educational and cultural trips.

- **Religious or Faith-Based Travel Clubs:** Organize pilgrimages, tours of religious sites, or other trips related to specific faiths.

Finding the right travel club can open doors to experiences you never imagined. Start by exploring online platforms like Meetup or Facebook groups dedicated to travel enthusiasts. These digital spaces are buzzing with recommendations and reviews, helping you identify clubs that align with your interests and travel style. Local senior centers and travel agencies are also valuable resources, often hosting informational sessions where you can meet club representatives and fellow travelers.

Before joining any travel club, it's essential to do your research:

- **Read Reviews:** Look for reviews from other members to get an idea of their experiences.

- **Ask Questions:** Don't hesitate to ask the club about their safety measures, cancellation policies, and any other concerns you have.

- **Compare Options:** Compare different travel clubs to find one that meets your needs and budget.

- **Prioritize Safety:** Reputable travel clubs prioritize the safety and well-being of their members. Here are some standard safety measures: Pre-Trip Information, including health advisories, local customs, and emergency contacts; Travel Insurance that covers medical expenses, trip cancellations, and other unforeseen events; 24/7 Support who can assist with any issues that arise during the trip; Emergency Plans with established procedures for handling medical emergencies, natural disasters, or other unforeseen events.

The benefits of joining a travel club extend beyond the destinations you visit. The friendship of fellow travelers enriches the journey, offering a sense of community and shared purpose. Group travel also provides an added layer of security and support, ensuring that you're never alone in navigating new environments.

Cost Comparison:

Comparing costs is tricky, as it depends heavily on the type of travel, destinations, and level of service. Here's a general overview:

- **Travel Clubs vs. Solo Travel:** Travel clubs often offer group discounts on flights, accommodation, and activities, which can make them more affordable than traveling solo, especially for luxury or specialized trips. However, for budget backpackers, solo travel may still be cheaper.

- **Travel Clubs vs. Other Group Tours:** Travel clubs may have a membership fee, but they often offer more flexibility and personalized experiences than extensive group tours. Smaller group sizes are also a benefit for some. The all-inclusive nature of some tours can make budgeting easier.

- **Consider "Value" not just "Cost":** Factor in the value of what's included (expert guides, special access, pre-planned itineraries) when comparing costs. Paying a bit more for a travel club offers a significantly better experience.

Consider the transformative power of travel clubs through real-life experiences. Take the story of a retiree who embarked on her first solo international trip, a journey that was daunting yet liberating. Joining a travel club offered her the support and encouragement she needed, transforming apprehension into excitement. As she explored new cultures and landscapes, she found herself building confidence and forming friendships that made her trip. Another group of travelers set off on a trip to a national park, where the beauty of nature served as the backdrop for unforgettable moments. Together, they hiked trails, shared meals under starlit skies, and forged connections that turned a simple trip into a cherished memory. These stories illustrate how travel clubs can enhance the travel experience, offering not just destinations but also a community that shares in the joy of discovery.

The beauty of travel clubs lies in their ability to transform travel from a solitary endeavor into a communal adventure. They provide opportunities to explore the world in a way that is both enriching and accessible, catering to a variety of interests and preferences. Whether you're venturing close to home or across the globe, a travel club can offer the perfect balance of structure and spontaneity, ensuring that every journey is filled with exploration, discovery, and friendship.

Adventure with a Purpose: Volunteer Travel

Imagine the thrill of exploring new destinations while simultaneously giving back to the communities you visit. Volunteer travel offers this unique combination, allowing you to immerse yourself in a culture while making meaningful contributions. It's not just about seeing new places; it's about becoming a part of them, even if only for a short while. Imagine working alongside locals in a bustling village, sharing stories and laughter, all while contributing to a cause that benefits the community. Whether it's helping build a school, teaching English, or participating in a conservation project, every effort leaves a positive impact. Volunteering abroad allows you to engage with cultures in a way that typical tourism doesn't, creating experiences and memories that last a lifetime.

Selecting the right volunteer vacation program involves some research, but the rewards are worth the effort. Start by identifying organizations known for their reputable programs, ensuring they align with your values and interests. Consider what you're passionate about — whether it's education, community-based conservation projects, infrastructure development, healthcare, microfinance projects, disaster relief and recovery, or environmental conservation — and choose a project that resonates with you. Many programs offer a variety of opportunities, so you're bound to find one that fits your skills and interests. Websites and reviews can provide insights into the experiences of past volunteers, giving you a clearer picture of what each program entails. Beware of "Orphanage Tourism": Volunteering at orphanages can unintentionally do more harm than good. Be very cautious of organizations that offer this type of experience. It's essential to choose a project that not only excites you but also allows you to contribute meaningfully.

Reputable Volunteer Travel Organizations:

It's crucial to choose an organization that aligns with your values and operates ethically. Here are some well-regarded options, but always do your own thorough research:

- **Global Vision International (GVI):** This organization offers a wide range of volunteer projects in various countries, focusing on conservation, community development, and wildlife protection. It is known for its responsible and sustainable approach.

- **Projects Abroad:** A large organization with diverse projects, from teaching and childcare to conservation and healthcare. Offers structured programs and comprehensive support.

- **International Volunteer HQ (IVHQ):** This organization connects volunteers with local organizations in developing countries. It offers affordable programs and a wide range of project options.

- **Cross-Cultural Solutions:** Focuses on community development projects, emphasizing cultural exchange and sustainable impact.

- **Earthwatch Institute:** This organization engages volunteers in scientific research projects around the world, contributing to conservation and environmental understanding.

- **Habitat for Humanity:** Offers opportunities to volunteer on home-building projects in the US and internationally.

- **United Planet:** Provides volunteer programs abroad with a focus on cultural immersion and community engagement.

- **Roadmonkey:** Combines adventure travel with volunteer work, often in remote or underserved communities.

Participating in volunteer travel offers numerous benefits beyond the immediate impact on the community. You have the chance to develop new skills or hone existing ones, all while making a difference. Imagine learning how to construct a water filtration system in a developing region or gaining experience in sustainable farming practices. These skills not only enrich your personal growth but also enhance your ability to contribute to future projects. The friendships formed with locals and fellow volunteers add depth to the experience. As you work side-by-side, cultural exchange occurs naturally, fostering cross-cultural friendships and understanding. These connections often extend beyond the project, becoming cherished relationships that broaden your global perspective.

Consider the retiree who spent months teaching English in a rural community in Japan where the language barrier was initially daunting. Through perseverance and creativity, bridges were built, and mutual understanding flourished. This experience not only enhanced her teaching skills but also deepened her appreciation for cultural diversity. Or think of the volunteer who joined an Amazon wildlife conservation project, helping protect endangered species and their habitats. The hands-on work with animals and the collaboration with conservationists made a tangible impact on environmental preservation. These stories demonstrate how volunteer travel can transform both the volunteer and the community, creating a legacy of change and connection.

Remember, the most impactful volunteer experiences are well-planned, ethically sound, and focused on empowering local communities. By choosing a reputable organization and approaching your experience with respect and a genuine desire to contribute, you can make a real difference.

Wrap-Up: Pack Your Bags

As you stand on the threshold of countless adventures, consider each trip as an opportunity to ignite your curiosity and expand your horizons. The world is a vast array of experiences waiting for your personal touch. Each journey can be a chapter in the story you wish to tell, a tale of discovery and joy that adds color and depth to your life. Whether you find yourself drawn to the vibrant pulse of a bustling city abroad or the serene tranquility of a quiet hamlet nearby, let your curiosity guide you. Embrace the spirit of exploration, knowing that each step you take is a step toward enriching your understanding of the world and your place within it.

Now is the perfect time to plan your next adventure. Start by setting your sights on a destination that excites your imagination, whether it's a local treasure you've yet to uncover or an international retreat that promises new perspectives. Consider the logistics: what mode of transport will bring you the most joy and convenience? Will you travel solo, or do you envision sharing the experience with friends or loved ones? Each choice shapes your journey, making it uniquely yours. Allow your plans to be as detailed or spontaneous as you wish, but be sure to leave room for the unexpected delights that travel so often brings. These moments usually become the highlights of any trip, the stories you share with laughter and fondness.

Remember, travel is not merely about the places you visit but the transformation it inspires within. Each experience adds to your understanding of the world, deepening your empathy and broadening your perspective. From the people you meet to the cultures you explore; every interaction holds potential for growth and connection. Traveling invites you to step outside your comfort zone, challenging you to see the world through fresh eyes and an open heart. It's a reminder that the world, in all its diversity and beauty, is accessible and welcoming to those willing to explore it.

As you prepare to set off on your next adventure, consider the impact of your travels. Embrace practices that honor the places you visit, from supporting local businesses to respecting cultural customs and traditions. These mindful choices not only enhance your experience but also contribute positively to the communities you encounter. Responsible travel ensures that the beauty and integrity of each destination remain intact for future explorers like yourself. It's about leaving each place a little better than you found it, creating a legacy of kindness and respect.

In this chapter, we've explored various avenues for adventure, from the intimacy of local discoveries to the expansive possibilities of international travel. Each offers its own set of rewards, enriching your life with stories and friendships that linger long after you return home. As you close this chapter, carry with you the excitement of what's to come. The world is vast, and the paths before you are many. Let your heart and curiosity be your guide, leading you toward experiences that inspire and fulfill. Your next adventure is just around the corner, ready to unfold with all the wonder and joy travel can bring.

CHAPTER FIVE

Fit for Life

Think of your body as a well-loved car. Over the years, it's driven countless miles, seen many roads, and carried you through life's twists and turns. Like any vehicle, it needs maintenance to keep running smoothly. Just as regular oil changes and tune-ups ensure a car's longevity, staying active is crucial for your health and well-being. The beauty of this stage of life is that you have the time to invest in yourself to make sure your engine keeps purring for years to come. So, how do we do that without revving the engine too hard?

Keep Moving

As we age, staying active isn't just about maintaining our physical health; it's a cornerstone of overall well-being. Regular movement helps keep your heart strong, your joints limber, and your mind sharp. You don't need to run marathons or lift heavy weights to achieve these benefits. In fact, low-impact activities can offer immense advantages, striking a balance between exertion and enjoyment. Picture a gentle morning walk where the sunlight filters through the trees or a leisurely bike ride by the lake. These activities improve cardiovascular health and help you maintain mobility, allowing you to move with ease and confidence.

We know what we should do, but how can we overcome the mental barriers to exercise?

- **Start Small:** Don't try to do too much too soon. Begin with short workouts and gradually increase the duration and intensity.

- **Find an Activity You Enjoy:** Choose activities that you find fun and engaging. You're more likely to stick with something you enjoy.

- **Set Realistic Goals:** Set achievable goals that you can realistically meet. Celebrate your successes along the way.

- **Schedule Your Workouts:** Treat your workouts like any other necessary appointment and schedule them in your calendar.

- **Find a Workout Buddy:** Exercising with a friend can provide motivation and accountability.

- **Reward Yourself:** After each workout, give yourself a small reward, like a healthy snack or a relaxing bath.

- **Don't Let Setbacks Derail You:** Everyone has days when they miss a workout. Don't let it discourage you. Just get back on track the next day.

- **Focus on How You Feel:** Pay attention to how good you feel after exercising. This positive feeling can be a powerful motivator.

- **Change Your Mindset:** Instead of thinking of exercise as a chore, consider it an investment in your health and well-being.

- **Visualize Success:** Imagine yourself achieving your fitness goals. This can help you stay motivated.

- **Seek Support:** If you're struggling to overcome mental barriers to exercise, talk to your doctor, a personal trainer, or a therapist.

Exercise isn't just a physical endeavor; it's a mental one too. Engaging in regular activity can significantly reduce stress levels, lift your mood, and boost emotional well-being. When you move, your body releases endorphins, those feel-good chemicals that elevate your spirits. It's like a natural mood booster, a way to shake off the day's stress and find a sense of calm. Whether it's a series of gentle stretches or a rhythmic dance session in your living room, these moments of movement provide a mental refresh, a chance to clear your mind, and reset your outlook.

Cognitive benefits are another compelling reason to stay active. Studies have shown that regular exercise can enhance brain function, improving memory and cognitive performance. It's like giving your brain a workout, strengthening your mental muscles alongside your physical ones. Think of it to keep your mind agile, ready to tackle puzzles, learn new skills, or engage in lively conversations. The mind-body connection is powerful and nurturing, and both ensure you're equipped to enjoy life's adventures, big or small.

Take a moment to reflect on the types of activities that resonate with you. Is it the tranquility of yoga or the camaraderie of a group class? It's the solitude of a morning walk or the rhythm of a dance. Write down what excites you about moving and how you can incorporate it into your routine. Consider setting a simple goal, like dedicating 30 minutes a day to an activity you love, and notice how it enhances your daily life.

As you explore ways to keep moving, remember that the goal isn't intensity but consistency. It's about finding joy in the activity, appreciating the way your body moves, and embracing the vitality it brings. There's no one-size-fits-all approach; it's about finding what works for you and making it a part of your lifestyle. Whether it's gentle stretching, a stroll through the park, or a fun fitness class, the key is to keep moving, to keep living with energy and enthusiasm.

Step by Step: Walking Clubs

Imagine the simple pleasure of putting one foot in front of the other, feeling the rhythm of your steps beating with the world around you. Walking is an exercise as old as time, yet its benefits are timeless. It's accessible, requiring nothing more than a pair of comfortable shoes and the desire to explore. Walking supports cardiovascular health, enhances mental clarity, and improves joint mobility. It's a gentle way to stay active, with low barriers to entry. Whether you choose to wander through local parks, meander along nature trails, or stroll along urban sidewalks, each step is a journey toward better health. Walking allows you to move at your own pace, savoring the scenery and the tranquility it brings. It's a versatile activity that can be done alone or in the company of friends, each step a testament to the body's enduring strength.

Joining a walking club can enhance this simple pleasure, transforming it into a shared experience. Community centers and online platforms often host existing groups, each providing a welcoming space for walkers of all abilities. If you can't find a club nearby, consider starting your own. Reach out to neighbors, post on social media, or put up flyers in local cafes. Set a regular schedule and choose routes that offer variety and interest. Walking clubs offer not only companionship but also motivation, as members encourage one another to meet regularly and celebrate each other's progress. This shared commitment creates bonds that extend beyond the trails, fostering friendships that enrich your life.

Adding goals to your walking routine can make the experience even more rewarding. Consider using a pedometer or fitness tracker to count your steps and setting daily or weekly targets to challenge yourself. Listening to music, podcasts, or audiobooks can accompany your walks, turning each outing into an opportunity for entertainment or learning. Explore scenic routes that change with the seasons, offering new sights and sounds to discover. Choose a historical theme for your walks, explore landmarks, and learn about the local area's past. Each walk can become an adventure, a chance to see the world through fresh eyes.

Here are some of my favorite walking apps:

Many apps can make your walks more fun and engaging:

- **Strava:** Tracks your walks, provides data on your pace and distance, and allows you to connect with other walkers.

- **MapMyWalk:** Similar to Strava, MapMyWalk offers route tracking, performance analysis, and social features. (I have learned all sorts of new parts of my neighborhood using this app. It's very fun!)

- **Walkmeter:** A comprehensive walking app that tracks your pace, distance, calories burned, and other metrics.

- **Zombies, Run!:** A fun and immersive app that turns your walk into a zombie-themed adventure.

- **Pokémon Go:** An augmented reality game that encourages you to walk to find and catch Pokémon.

- **Audible or Podcasts:** Listen to audiobooks or podcasts while you walk to make the time pass more quickly (Radiolab is my all-time favorite podcast).

- **Music Apps (Spotify, Pandora, Apple Music):** Create a walking playlist with upbeat music to keep you motivated.

The stories of those who have embraced walking clubs are as varied as the paths they tread. One member spoke of how regular walks helped her shed pounds and regain energy, while another found solace in the simple act of walking after a stressful day. Friendships formed on these trails often extend into other areas of life, with club members organizing social events and supporting each other through life's ups and downs. Walking clubs offer more than just exercise; they provide a community and a sense of belonging that strengthens both body and soul.

Safety is paramount when walking, and a few simple precautions can ensure your comfort and well-being. Choose supportive shoes that cushion your feet and provide stability. Apply sunscreen to protect your skin, even on cloudy days, and wear a hat or sunglasses for added protection. Stay hydrated by carrying a water bottle, especially on warmer days. Pay attention to your body's signals and walk at a pace that feels comfortable. If you experience discomfort or fatigue, it's okay to pause and rest. Walking is about enjoyment and well-being, not competition. By taking these steps, you can walk your way to wellness, one step at a time.

Making a Splash: Water Aerobics

Imagine yourself stepping into a pool, the water gently hugging your body, offering buoyant support as you move. Water aerobics is more than exercise; it's a refreshing escape that combines fitness with fun, all while being gentle on the joints. For seniors, water aerobics presents a fantastic opportunity to engage in effective cardiovascular and muscle-building workouts without the strain that traditional exercises might impose. The buoyancy of water diminishes the impact on your joints, allowing you to enjoy a full range of motion with ease. The resistance that water naturally provides means your muscles are constantly working, enhancing strength and endurance. This is hands down one of the best exercise options, offering a supportive environment in which to stay active without worrying about injury.

Health Conditions Improved by Water Aerobics:

Water aerobics is a fantastic low-impact exercise option with numerous health benefits, beneficial for individuals with certain conditions or limitations:

- **Arthritis:** Water's buoyancy reduces joint stress, making water aerobics ideal for people with arthritis. It can improve joint mobility, reduce pain, and increase strength.

- **Osteoarthritis:** Like arthritis, the reduced weight-bearing in water eases joint pain and stiffness associated with osteoarthritis.

- **Back Pain:** Water's buoyancy supports the spine, reducing pressure and allowing gentle movements that can strengthen back muscles and improve flexibility.

- **Obesity:** Water aerobics provides a calorie-burning workout without the high impact of land-based exercises, making it a suitable option for individuals working to lose weight.

- **Joint Injuries:** Water exercise can be a great way to rehabilitate after joint injuries, as it allows for movement without putting excessive stress on healing tissues.

- **Multiple Sclerosis (MS):** The cooling effect of water

can be soothing for people with MS, and buoyancy can assist with balance and movement.

- **Fibromyalgia:** Water's warmth and gentle resistance can help ease pain and stiffness associated with fibromyalgia, while exercise can improve overall fitness.

- **Cardiovascular Conditions:** Water aerobics can improve cardiovascular health without putting excessive strain on the heart.

- **Balance Issues:** The water provides support and reduces the risk of falls, making water aerobics a safe way to improve balance and coordination.

- **Limited Mobility:** Water's buoyancy can make movements more manageable for those with limited mobility, allowing them to participate in exercises they might not be able to do on land.

Finding a water aerobics class is an excellent way to incorporate this beneficial activity into your routine. Local pools and fitness centers often offer courses tailored to varying fitness levels. Typically, lessons begin with a warm-up to prepare your body, followed by cardiovascular exercises designed to get your heart pumping. As you move through the water, you'll engage in routines that may include jogging, leg lifts, and arm movements, all aimed at building strength and improving flexibility. The session usually concludes with a cool-down period, allowing your body to relax and recover. These classes provide a structured approach to fitness, ensuring you get a comprehensive workout that's both challenging and enjoyable.

Beyond the physical benefits, water aerobics offers a vibrant community experience. Participating in group classes fosters connections, making exercise a social event rather than a solitary task. The shared experience of moving through the water and encouraging each other creates friendships. You'll find that the support and motivation from fellow class members can make all the difference in maintaining regular attendance and achieving your fitness goals. Whether you're sharing a laugh over a particularly challenging routine or celebrating each other's progress, the social aspect of water aerobics improves the experience, turning every class into a gathering of friends.

Consider the inspiring stories of those who have found renewed vitality through water aerobics. One senior, after knee surgery, discovered that water aerobics not only aided in her rehabilitation but also transformed her outlook on exercise. She found joy in the rhythmic movements, her pain diminished, and over time, her mobility improved significantly. Another participant, initially hesitant to join a group class, found that the water offered a sense of freedom and comfort, allowing her to move without fear of falling or injury. These individuals are just a few examples of how water aerobics has positively impacted lives, providing both physical and emotional benefits.

Safety is a key consideration when engaging in any exercise, and water aerobics is no exception. Staying hydrated is crucial, even when exercising in water, as you might not realize how much you're sweating. Listening to your body is equally important; if you feel fatigued or uncomfortable, it's okay to take a break. Avoid overexertion by pacing yourself and adjusting movements to suit your comfort level. Water provides a safe environment, but it's essential to ensure your safety by being mindful of your limits. With these precautions, water aerobics can be a safe, effective, and enjoyable way to stay active. Go make a splash!

Dance Your Way to Fitness

Imagine a room filled with music, your feet tapping to the rhythm, and a sense of joy sweeping over you as you move.

Dance, in all its forms, is more than just a physical activity; it's an expression of life itself. Whether you find yourself swaying in a ballroom or stepping to the beat in a line dancing class, dance offers a host of benefits that extend beyond physical. Moving to music can enhance your cardiovascular health, improving circulation and boosting heart function. It also sharpens balance and coordination, encouraging your body to work in harmony. Stretching and bending during dance routines enhance flexibility, while the mental focus required to remember steps and sequences stimulates cognitive function. The magic of dance lies not only in its ability to keep your body fit but also in its power to uplift your spirit, bringing a smile to your face and a lift to your mood.

When it comes to choosing the right dance style, the possibilities are as varied as the genres of music you love. The elegance of ballroom dancing calls to you with its graceful movements and structured steps. Or the infectious energy of salsa, with its lively rhythms and spirited spins, is more your style. Line dancing offers a social and approachable option, with easy-to-follow steps that invite everyone to join in the fun. For those looking for a modern twist, Zumba Gold offers a high-energy workout tailored specifically for seniors, combining dance and fitness in a way that's accessible and enjoyable. When selecting a style, consider your interests and physical abilities. Many community centers and dance schools offer beginner classes, ensuring you can find a pace and style that suits you. The most important thing is to choose a dance form that excites you and makes you want to move.

Most popular dance classes for seniors:

The availability of specific dance styles will vary based on your location but don't forget that there are a ton of online tutorial options. Here are some standard options and where to look:

- **Ballroom Dance (Waltz, Tango, Foxtrot, Swing):** Often offered at dance studios, community centers, or senior centers. Look for classes specifically labeled "beginner" or "introductory."

- **Latin Dance (Salsa, Cha-Cha, Rumba, Merengue):** Check dance studios, community centers, or cultural centers. Some studios specialize in Latin dance.

- **Line Dancing:** Popular in senior centers and community events. No partner is needed!

- **Folk Dance:** Many communities have folk dance groups that welcome beginners. These dances are often simple and repetitive, making them easy to learn.

- **Social Dance:** This can encompass a variety of partner dances, often taught in a casual and social setting.

- **Ballet (Beginner/Adult Ballet):** Some dance studios offer adult ballet classes for beginners, focusing on basic technique and movement. These classes are great for working on balance and flexibility.

- **Jazz/Modern Dance (Beginner/Adult):** Like ballet, some studios may have introductory classes for adults.

- **Tap Dance (Beginner/Adult):** Tap is a fun and energetic style that can be adapted for beginners. Cardio with a smile!

- **Hip Hop/Street Dance (Beginner/Adult):** Some studios may offer beginner hip-hop or street dance classes for adults.

Dance is a social activity at its core, an excellent way to meet new people and create lasting friendships. Whether you attend a class with a partner or go solo, dance invites you to connect with others who share your passion for movement. The shared experience of learning new steps and mastering routines fosters camaraderie, turning classmates into friends. Couples dance classes can strengthen connections and offer a fun way to expand your horizons with your partner, while solo courses allow you to focus on your personal growth and enjoyment. Dance festivals and performance groups provide further avenues for social engagement, offering opportunities to travel, perform, and celebrate the joy of dance with others. Imagine the excitement of participating in a local dance showcase or attending a festival where you can watch and learn from dancers of all levels.

Consider the stories of those who have found joy and fulfillment in dance. One individual, having never danced before retirement, joined a local salsa class and discovered a newfound confidence and zest for life. Another, a former ballet dancer, reignited their passion by joining a seniors' performance group, traveling to festivals, and sharing the stage with friends. These stories highlight the transformative power of dance, showing us that it's never too late to embrace the rhythm of life and find happiness on the dance floor.

Safety is essential when dancing, and there are a few key tips to keep in mind to ensure a safe and enjoyable experience. Always start with a warm-up to prepare your muscles and joints, reducing the risk of strain or injury. Listen to your body and pace yourself, especially if you're new to dancing or trying a more vigorous style. Take breaks when needed and modify movements to suit your comfort level. It's about enjoying the process, not pushing yourself beyond your limits. By approaching dance with care and enthusiasm, you can enjoy all the benefits it has to offer, from improved fitness to newfound friendships. Dance is a celebration of life, an invitation to move, connect, and feel fabulous every step of the way.

Pedaling into Retirement

Imagine the wind in your hair, the sun on your face, and the rhythmic whir of your bicycle wheels as you explore scenic paths and discover hidden gems in your community. Cycling in retirement offers a delightful blend of exercise, adventure, and connection with the outdoors. It's a chance to rediscover the simple pleasure of two wheels, combined with the freedom to explore at your own pace. For seniors, cycling presents a fantastic opportunity to engage in low-impact cardiovascular exercise that strengthens muscles, improves balance, and boosts overall well-being, all without the jarring impact that other activities might impose. The gentle motion of pedaling is kind to joints, allowing you to enjoy a full range of motion while building endurance and stamina. This form of exercise is particularly beneficial if you've experienced joint pain or have conditions like arthritis, offering a supportive way to stay active and mobile.

Here are some popular bike options:

- **Comfort Bikes:** Designed for relaxed, upright riding. They typically have wider tires for stability, comfy table saddles, and swept-back handlebars that reduce strain on the back and wrists. They are great for paved paths and gentle trails.

- **Hybrid Bikes:** A versatile option that combines features of road and mountain bikes. They're suitable for paved paths, gravel roads, and some light trails. A good balance between comfort and efficiency.

- **Electric Bikes (E-bikes):** These bikes have a small motor that assists while driving. They can be invaluable for seniors who want to ride longer distances or tackle hills with less effort. E-bikes can make cycling accessible to those with varying fitness levels.

- **Recumbent Bikes:** These bikes allow the rider to sit

in a reclined position, which can be more comfortable for some seniors, especially those with back problems. They offer good stability and can be easier on the joints.

- **Tricycles (Trikes):** Trikes offer excellent stability and are a good option for seniors who are concerned about balance. They can be a great way to enjoy cycling without fear of falling.

Finding a bike route that suits your fitness level and interest is an excellent way to begin this rewarding activity. Local parks and recreation departments often maintain networks of bike paths, offering smooth, paved surfaces ideal for leisurely rides. Rails-to-trails conversions, utilizing the former railway lines, provide scenic, relatively flat routes that wind through picturesque landscapes. Exploring these local resources allows you to discover hidden corners of your community, from quiet wooded trails to lively waterfront areas. Planning your route and considering the distance, terrain, and available amenities ensures a safe and enjoyable experience.

Beyond the physical benefits, biking offers a unique opportunity for social engagement. Joining a local cycling club or simply inviting a friend to join you on a ride can transform exercise into a shared adventure. The company of fellow cyclists, the exchange of tips and encouragement, and the shared experience of exploring the open road create lasting friendships. You'll find that the support and motivation from fellow riders can make all the difference in maintaining a regular cycling routine and achieving your fitness goals. Whether you're sharing stories during a rest stop or celebrating a scenic vista, the social aspect of biking enriches the experience, turning every ride into a gathering of friends.

Consider the inspiring stories of those who have embraced biking in their retirement years. One senior, after years of sedentary living, discovered a newfound passion for cycling,

rediscovering the joy of movement and the thrill of exploration. She found that it not only improved her physical
health but also boosted her confidence and sense of well-being. Another retiree, who was initially hesitant to join a group,
found that the shared experience of riding alongside others
created a sense of belonging and connection, transforming
his perspective on exercise. These individuals are just a few
examples of how cycling has positively impacted lives, providing both physical and emotional benefits.

Safety is a key consideration when engaging in any physical
activity, and cycling is no exception. Wearing a helmet is
crucial for protecting your head in case of a fall. Regularly
checking your bike's brakes, tires, and other components
ensures a safe riding experience. Being aware of your surroundings, obeying traffic laws, and using hand signals when
turning are essential for navigating shared paths and roads.
Choosing routes that are appropriate for your fitness level
and avoiding extreme weather conditions are also necessary
safety precautions. With these considerations, cycling can
be a safe, effective, and enjoyable way to stay active and
engaged in your retirement years.

Dinking for Fun: Pickleball

Imagine yourself stepping onto a court, paddle in hand,
ready to engage in a fast-paced, social, and surprisingly ad-
dictive game. Pickleball, a sport that combines elements of
tennis, badminton, and table tennis, is more than just a
recreational activity; it's a vibrant and engaging way to stay
active and connected in retirement. For seniors, pickleball offers a fantastic opportunity to enjoy a low-impact cardiovascular workout that enhances agility, improves reflexes, and
boosts overall fitness, all while being gentle on the joints.

The smaller court size compared to tennis reduces the
amount of running required, making it a less strenuous
option for those seeking an active lifestyle. The underhand

serve and the nature of the game minimize stress on shoulders and other joints, allowing you to enjoy a full range of motion with less risk of injury. This sport is particularly beneficial if you've experienced joint pain or have conditions like arthritis, offering a supportive environment to stay active and mobile.

Finding a pickleball court or group is an excellent way to incorporate this beneficial activity into your routine. Local recreation centers, community parks, and even some senior centers often have dedicated pickleball courts or organize regular play sessions. Many communities are seeing a surge in pickleball popularity, leading to new courts and programs popping up regularly. Checking with your local parks and recreation department or searching online for "pickleball near me" can connect you with local resources.

Here are some great online resources to learn more:

- **USA Pickleball Association (USAPA):** The USAPA website (usapickleball.org) is an excellent resource. They have information on rules and equipment and often list local clubs and places to play.

- **YouTube:** Numerous videos on YouTube offer beginner instructions, from basic rules and techniques to drills and strategies. Search for "pickleball lessons for beginners."

Typically, play sessions involve rotating partners, allowing you to meet and interact with a variety of players. Whether you're participating in a casual open play session or joining a more structured league, pickleball offers a fun and engaging way to stay active.

Beyond the physical benefits, pickleball offers a welcoming community experience. Participating in group play fosters a sense of comradery, making exercise a social event rather than a solitary task. The shared experience of friendly competition, the exchange of tips and encouragement, and the shared laughter over a particularly well-placed "dink" create lasting friendships. Whether you're celebrating a winning point or commiserating over a missed shot, the social aspect of pickleball enriches the experience, turning every game into a gathering of friends.

Consider the inspiring stories of those who have discovered renewed vitality through pickleball. One senior found that pickleball provided a perfect outlet for staying active and engaged. She discovered a newfound passion for the sport, improving her fitness level and making new friends in the process. Another participant, initially hesitant to try a new sport, found that pickleball offered a sense of accomplishment and joy, boosting her confidence and overall well-being. These individuals are just a few examples of how pickleball has positively impacted lives, providing both physical and emotional benefits.

Safety is a key consideration when engaging in any physical activity, and pickleball is no exception. Wearing appropriate athletic shoes that provide good traction and support can help prevent slips and falls. Staying hydrated is crucial, especially during longer play sessions. Listening to your body is equally important; if you feel fatigued or uncomfortable, it's okay to take a break. Avoiding overexertion by pacing yourself and adjusting your level of play to suit your comfort level is also important. While pickleball is generally a low-impact sport, it's essential to be mindful of your physical limitations and to play within your abilities. With these precautions, pickleball can be a safe, effective, and enjoyable way to stay active and connected in your retirement years.

Wrap-Up: Fit for the Future

Imagine the dawn of a new morning, the day stretching before you with untapped potential. In the same way, committing to lifelong wellness is like a gentle awakening, a dedication to keeping your body and mind vibrant and ready for the adventures ahead. As we embrace retirement, the importance of staying active cannot be overstated. It isn't about chasing youth but about enhancing the life we have, ensuring that our later years are filled with vitality and joy. Participating in regular fitness activities can safeguard our independence, allowing us to live with confidence and ease. Whether it's stretching in the morning sun, enjoying a leisurely bike ride, or participating in a community class, these moments of movement add up, creating a solid foundation of health and well-being.

The goal here is not a grueling workout regimen but a lifestyle that integrates activity in a way that feels natural and enjoyable. What we're aiming for is a balance that keeps us energized and engaged, helping to ward off health issues and enhance our quality of life. Think of it as an investment in a future where you can stand tall, move freely, and enjoy all that life has to offer. To start, consider what makes you feel alive. Is it the movement of a dance, the calm focus of yoga, or perhaps the camaraderie of a group class? Choose activities that resonate with you, ones that bring a smile to your face and a spring to your step. By aligning your pursuits with your interests, you're more likely to stick with them, reaping the benefits of consistency over time.

Starting small and staying consistent is key. Begin with activities that align with your current abilities, gradually building up as you grow more confident and capable. Maybe it's a short walk around your neighborhood or a few minutes of stretching each morning. Over time, these small efforts compound, creating a foundation for long-term health benefits. Consistency doesn't mean rigidity, though. It's essential to remain flexible, allowing your routine to evolve as your interests and needs change. Perhaps you'll discover a new passion or rekindle an old one. Embrace these shifts as opportunities for growth and exploration, keeping your wellness journey dynamic and fulfilling.

Consider the impact that such a commitment can have on your life. Staying active not only enhances physical health but also contributes to mental clarity and emotional balance. It's about creating a life you love, one that's filled with moments of joy and satisfaction. When you prioritize wellness, you're not just adding years to your life; you're adding life to your years. It's a path to independence, strength, and a sense of purpose, allowing you to engage fully with the world around you. There's a particular joy in knowing that you're doing what you can to stay fit for the future, ready to take on whatever comes your way.

As we wrap up this chapter, let's carry forward the knowledge that each step, no matter how small, moves us toward a healthier, more vibrant life. The journey of wellness is a lifelong endeavor, one that enriches every moment and enhances our capacity to enjoy the beauty and wonder of the world. With enthusiasm and commitment, we can cultivate a fulfilling and active retirement, one that reflects our desires and dreams. Now, as we turn the page, let's look ahead with optimism, ready to embrace the next chapter of our lives with open hearts and open minds.

CHAPTER SIX

Nature Calls

P icture the serene rustle of leaves in a gentle breeze, the sun peeking through the branches, casting a warm glow on your face. Close your eyes for a moment and imagine the earthy scent of a forest after a light rain. These simple pleasures are nature's invitation to step outside and explore its wonders. As you embark on retirement, the great outdoors offers endless possibilities for adventure, relaxation, and connection. It's a call to rediscover the beauty of nature, to let its calming presence nourish your spirit and invigorate your senses and soul. Whether it's the sound of birdsong at dawn or the sight of a flower blooming in your garden, nature has a unique way of grounding us, reminding us of life's simple joys.

Nature's Remedy

Consider the transformative power of nature and its ability to enhance your physical, mental, and emotional well-being. Spending time outdoors is not just about enjoying a pleasant day; it's about embracing a lifestyle that promotes health and happiness. Engaging in outdoor activities can help maintain your mobility, improve your balance, and strengthen your muscles. Even a leisurely walk in the park can elevate your heart rate, boosting cardiovascular health without the need for strenuous exercise. The fresh air and sunlight invigorate the body and mind, providing a natural remedy for fatigue and encouraging a positive outlook on life.

Mentally, nature's influence is profound. The simple act of being surrounded by greenery can significantly reduce stress levels, soothe anxiety, and enhance mood. Nature fosters a sense of peace and tranquility, allowing you to unwind and escape from the hustle and bustle of daily life. The sights, sounds, and smells of the outdoors engage your senses, offering a form of therapy that rejuvenates the mind. Studies have shown that exposure to natural environments can even improve cognitive function and concentration, keeping the mind sharp and resilient as you age.

The social benefits of outdoor activities are equally compelling. Nature provides a setting for community and connection, whether you're part of a gardening club, a hiking group, or simply enjoying a picnic with friends. These activities offer opportunities to meet new people, share experiences, and connect over shared interests. The shared joy of exploring a new trail or planting a garden fosters friendships and creates lasting memories. Engaging with others in outdoor settings can combat feelings of isolation and loneliness, enriching your social life and enhancing your overall sense of well-being.

Exploring hobbies like bird watching, gardening, and nature walks can deepen your connection with the natural world while promoting physical activity and social interaction. Bird watching is a simple yet rewarding activity that invites you to observe the grace and beauty of our feathered friends. All you need is a pair of binoculars and a field guide to get started. Bird watching encourages mindfulness and patience, allowing you to immerse yourself in the serene rhythms of nature. It's an activity that can be enjoyed alone or with others, providing a peaceful way to connect with the environment and fellow bird enthusiasts.

Gardening offers a hands-on approach to engaging with nature, allowing you to cultivate your own little paradise. Whether you have a spacious backyard or a cozy balcony, gardening brings the benefits of fresh air and physical activity right on your doorstep. The act of tending to plants, watching them grow and flourish under your care, is deeply satisfying and can provide a sense of purpose and accomplishment. Gardening also supports biodiversity, attracting beneficial insects like bees and butterflies, contributing to the health of our planet.

Nature walks offer a chance to explore diverse landscapes, from local parks and reserves to hidden trails and scenic spots. Each walk presents an opportunity to witness the beauty of seasonal changes, from the vibrant colors of autumn leaves to the delicate blooms of spring. Whether it's a short stroll or a more challenging hike, nature walks provide a gentle form of exercise that boosts physical health while offering moments of reflection and serenity. They also encourage social interaction, as you can join group hikes or guided walks to learn more about the local flora and fauna.

Take a moment to consider how you can incorporate more of nature into your life. Reflect on the activities that resonate with you, and think about how they can enrich your days. Whether it's a daily walk in the park, joining a community garden, or simply enjoying a cup of tea on your porch as the sun rises, these moments of connection with nature can be a source of joy and renewal. Keep a journal to document your experiences and observations, noting the changes in your mood and outlook as you spend more time outdoors. Let this reflection guide you in creating a lifestyle that embraces the healing power of nature, nurturing your body, mind, and spirit in retirement.

The Joy of Gardening

Imagine stepping into your garden, where the morning sun paints the world in soft hues, and the fresh scent of earth fills the air. This is your sanctuary, a place where you can cultivate beauty and nourish life. Whether it's the vibrant colors of blooming flowers or the satisfaction of harvesting your own vegetables, gardening offers a fulfilling way to engage with nature. It all begins with choosing the right location for your garden. Look for a sunny spot with good drainage, as sunlight is the lifeblood of most plants. Too much water, however, can drown their roots, so ensure the soil drains well. If you're unsure about your soil's health, a simple test can reveal its pH and nutrient levels, guiding you in creating the perfect environment for your plants to thrive.

Equipping yourself with the right tools is essential for any gardener. A sturdy trowel for digging and planting, sharp pruners for trimming, and a reliable watering can will serve you well. These basic tools become extensions of your hands, enabling you to care for your garden with ease. Consider starting with easy-to-grow plants, especially if you're new to gardening. Lettuce, tomatoes, marigolds, and herbs are all great options for beginners. They require minimal maintenance and reward you with quick results, boosting your confidence as you watch them flourish under your care. As you become more comfortable, you explore more challenging varieties, gradually expanding your garden's diversity.

Determining the Best Plants:

Knowing your climate is crucial for successful container gardening. Here's how to determine the best plants:

1. **Know Your USDA Plant Hardiness Zone:** This zone map divides the US into regions based on average minimum winter temperatures. It helps you determine which plants can survive the winter in your area. You can easily find your zone online by searching "USDA plant hardiness zone [your location]."

2. **Check Local Nurseries and Garden Centers:** They carry plants that are well-suited for the local climate. The staff can also offer valuable advice.

3. **Consult Local Gardening Resources:** Your local Co-operative Extension Service, botanical gardens, or gardening clubs can provide information on the best plants for your area.

4. **Read Plant Tags and Seed Packets:** These often include information about the plant's hardiness, light requirements, and watering needs.

5. **Consider Sun Exposure:** Observe how much sun your container garden receives. Choose plants that match the light conditions (full sun, partial shade, or full shade).

6. **Think About Water Needs:** Some plants require more water than others. Group plants with similar watering needs together to make watering easier.

7. **Choose the Right Size Plants:** Select plants that are appropriate for the size of your containers.

8. **Consider the Growing Season:** Some plants are best suited for spring planting, while others thrive in the summer or fall.

When it comes to the type of garden you want, the possibilities are endless. Vegetable gardens offer a way to grow your own food, providing fresh, organic produce right at your doorstep. Imagine the joy of picking a ripe tomato or a handful of leafy greens, knowing that your efforts have brought them to life. Not only do they save you a trip to the grocery store, but they also offer nutritional benefits that enhance your diet. Flower and herb gardens, on the other hand, transform your outdoor space into a vibrant oasis. The colors and fragrances invite relaxation, turning your garden into a haven of tranquility. Herbs add an aromatic touch, enhancing your culinary creations with flavors fresh from the garden.

For those with limited space, container gardening is a fantastic alternative. You don't need a sprawling yard to enjoy the benefits of gardening. Balconies, patios, and windowsills can become your oasis, where pots brim with life and color. Containers allow you to grow a variety of plants, from herbs like basil and mint to flowers and even vegetables like peppers and tomatoes. They offer flexibility, letting you move them to catch the sun or find shelter from the wind. This adaptability makes container gardening accessible to everyone, regardless of space constraints.

Gardening is not just about the plants; it's about the gardener, too. The physical act of gardening provides a low-impact exercise that can help keep you fit and flexible. Tasks like digging, bending, and weeding engage your muscles, promoting strength and mobility. But the benefits extend beyond the physical. Gardening can also be a meditative practice, a time for mindfulness and reflection. As you tend to your plants, the rhythmic nature of the work allows your mind to relax and unwind. It's a chance to disconnect from the stresses of daily life and reconnect with the present moment.

The environmental impact of gardening is another rewarding aspect to consider. By cultivating your own garden, you contribute to biodiversity, creating a habitat for beneficial insects like bees and butterflies. Your efforts help sustain these creatures, playing a small but significant part in preserving the ecosystem. Growing your own food reduces reliance on mass-produced crops, decreasing your carbon footprint and supporting a more sustainable lifestyle. Each plant you nurture is a step towards a healthier planet, making your garden a testament to environmental stewardship.

Maintaining your garden requires attention and care. Regular watering is crucial, especially during dry spells. Listen to your plants; they will tell you when they need more water. Pest control is another challenge, but it can be managed with organic methods. Consider using neem oil or companion planting to deter pests without harming the environment. These natural solutions protect your garden while maintaining its ecological balance. Gardening is a journey, one that transforms not only the landscape but the gardener as well. From changing small spaces into lush gardens to reaping the rewards of homegrown produce, the joy of gardening is boundless.

Sowing Seeds of Friendship: Community Gardens

Imagine a sunny morning, the air crisp and inviting, as you greet fellow gardeners with a warm smile. Around you, the earth is alive with promise, each plot a testament to shared dreams and aspirations. Community gardening is more than just planting seeds—it's about cultivating friendships and nurturing a sense of belonging. When you step into a shared garden, you're not just tending to plants; you're directly contributing to a community. Working side-by-side, you and your fellow gardeners exchange tips, stories, and laughter, each interaction strengthening the roots of friendships. There's something uniquely satisfying about watching a garden flourish through collective effort; each bloom is a symbol of teamwork and fellowship. As you plant, water, and harvest together, you create not just a garden but a vibrant community where trust and friendship grow alongside the plants.

Finding community garden opportunities:

- **Checking with Local Organizations:**

    ◦ Local Councils or Municipalities (Parks & Recreation, Community Development, Social Services)

    ◦ Senior Centers or Community Centers

    ◦ Gardening or Horticultural Societies (local chapters)

    ◦ Environmental or Conservation Groups

    ◦ Religious Organizations

    ◦ Schools or Universities (community garden projects, workshops)

    ◦ Local Charities or Non-profits (food security, community development)

- **Searching Online:**

    ◦ Use location-specific keywords: "community gardens near [location]," "senior volunteer opportunities [location]," and "gardening clubs [location]."

    ◦ Add terms like "for seniors" or "volunteer opportunities" to refine searches.

- **Exploring Nearby Communities:**

    ◦ Consider expanding your search to neighboring towns or cities.

- **Utilizing Online Resources:**

- Community Garden Websites (e.g., communityg arden.org)

- Volunteer Websites (e.g., VolunteerMatch.org and similar platforms globally)

- **Networking with Others:**

  - Talk to neighbors and visit local markets (farmers' markets, produce stands).

  - Check community bulletin boards (libraries, cafes, community centers).

The benefits of community gardening extend beyond personal connections. These shared spaces often contribute to local sustainability by producing fresh, nutritious food for community members and local food banks. Imagine the pride of delivering baskets of homegrown vegetables to those in need, knowing your efforts have made a tangible difference. Community gardens also promote environmental stewardship, encouraging sustainable practices that benefit the planet. Techniques such as composting and rainwater harvesting are standard, turning garden waste into rich soil and capturing precious water resources. These methods not only enhance the garden's health but also model eco-friendly practices for the wider community, inspiring others to adopt sustainable habits.

Getting involved in a community garden is easy. Start by reaching out to local community centers or environmental organizations to learn about existing projects in your area. Many gardens welcome new members with open arms, eager to share the joy and responsibility of gardening. Attend meetings and events to familiarize yourself with the garden's goals. As you participate, you'll discover a wealth of opportunities to engage, from planning and planting to organizing events and workshops. Every contribution, no matter how small, enriches the community and solidifies your place within it.

Collaborative gardening is an enriching experience. Working on a shared plot enhances team spirit as everyone pitches in to create a thriving garden. This cooperation fosters a sense of unity and belonging, as each member's unique skills and perspectives contribute to the garden's success. Whether you're an experienced gardener or a novice, there's always something to learn and teach. The garden becomes a living classroom where knowledge is freely shared, and the joy of discovery is constant. As you work together, you'll find that the garden's growth mirrors the growth of your social connections, each leaf a testament to friendship and collaboration.

Sustainability is at the heart of community gardening. By implementing eco-friendly practices, these gardens become models of environmental responsibility. Composting transforms kitchen scraps and garden waste into nutrient-rich soil, reducing landfill waste and enriching the earth. Rainwater harvesting captures and stores rain, providing a sustainable water source that conserves precious resources. These practices not only benefit the garden but also demonstrate the power of collective action in addressing environmental challenges. Community gardens serve as beacons of hope and resilience, showing that when we come together, we can create positive change for ourselves and the planet.

Community gardens offer a sanctuary where you can connect with nature and people simultaneously. They provide a space to unwind, reflect, and engage in meaningful work. As you dig your hands into the soil, you'll find that the simple act of gardening can be profoundly therapeutic, soothing the mind and lifting the spirit. In these shared spaces, you'll encounter a wide variety of individuals, each bringing their own stories, experiences, and dreams. Together, you create a mosaic of humanity, vibrant and dynamic, united by a common purpose. Community gardening is a celebration of life, both botanical and human, where every seed planted is a promise of growth, and every harvest is a testament to the power of community.

The Call of the Wild: Bird Watching

Imagine sitting quietly in your backyard, the morning sun warming your face as the world wakes up around you. The gentle rustle of leaves is interrupted by the melodic chirping of birds, each note a reminder of nature's soundtrack. Bird watching is a simple yet profound way to connect with the natural world. It's an activity that requires little more than a curious eye and a willingness to pause and observe. Best of all, you can enjoy it almost anywhere — from the comfort of your yard to your favorite local park. The beauty of bird watching lies in its simplicity and accessibility. All you need is a pair of binoculars, a field guide to help identify the birds you see, and perhaps a birding app for the more tech-savvy among us. These tools open a world of discovery, turning each outing into an adventure filled with wonder and surprise.

Creating a bird-friendly environment at home can enhance your bird watching experience. Consider adding a bird feeder to attract a variety of species. Different seeds and feeders appeal to other birds, so a bit of experimentation might be needed. Bird baths can also draw in feathered visitors, offering them a place to drink and bathe. If you're feeling ambitious, plant native shrubs and flowers that provide natural food sources and shelter. These simple additions transform your space into a haven for local wildlife, inviting a vibrant array of birds to visit throughout the year. Watching them up close, you'll gain a deeper appreciation for their habits and personalities, each one a character in the unfolding drama of your backyard.

Best Bird Watching Apps:

- **Merlin Bird ID (Cornell Lab of Ornithology):** Excellent for identifying birds by photo, sound, or answering simple questions.

- **eBird (Cornell Lab of Ornithology):** A powerful tool for recording bird sightings, exploring hotspots, and contributing to citizen science.

- **Audubon Bird Guide:** Provides information on bird identification, behavior, and habitat.

- **Sibley Birds:** A detailed field guide app with beautiful illustrations and bird songs.

- **iBird Pro:** A comprehensive birding app with advanced search and filtering options.

Bird watching offers a unique form of mindfulness, encouraging you to slow down and focus on the present moment. The practice of identifying different species sharpens your observation skills and enhances your attention to detail. You learn to notice subtle distinctions in plumage, song, and behavior, engaging your brain in a delightful exercise that keeps it active and alert. This focus provides a welcome distraction from everyday concerns, offering a calming effect that reduces stress and promotes mental well-being. The serenity of the natural world, coupled with the quiet satisfaction of a successful sighting, brings a sense of peace and contentment.

The mental health benefits of bird watching are well-documented. Spending time in nature has been shown to alleviate anxiety and depression, and bird watching is no exception. The sense of accomplishment that comes from identifying a rare species or observing a new behavior can boost your mood and self-esteem. Tracking birds over time also provides a sense of continuity and purpose as you witness the changing seasons and migration patterns. Each new sighting becomes a cherished memory, a testament to the beauty and resilience of the natural world.

Bird watching is not just a solitary pursuit. It offers opportunities for social connection and shared experiences. Joining a local bird watching group or club can introduce you to fellow enthusiasts who share your passion. These groups often organize outings and events, providing a platform to learn and grow together. Sharing your observations with others enriches the experience as you exchange tips, stories, and sightings. The friendship that blossoms in these communities adds more joy to bird watching, turning a solitary hobby into a communal celebration of nature. Not only do you learn from each other, but you also build friendships based on a shared love for nature's creatures.

Embarking on bird watching adventures can lead to some truly memorable encounters. Imagine the thrill of spotting a rare migratory species or witnessing a spectacular mating display. These moments are awe-inspiring, reminding us of the wonder and diversity of life on our planet. Bird watching trips can take you to breathtaking destinations, from serene wetlands to lush forests, each teeming with avian life. Whether it's a weekend trip to a nearby nature reserve or an organized tour with experienced guides, these adventures deepen your connection to the natural world and fuel your passion for preserving it.

Bird watching is a gentle reminder of the interconnectedness of all living things. It fosters a sense of stewardship for the environment, inspiring us to protect and cherish the habitats that sustain these beautiful creatures. In this way, bird watching becomes more than just a hobby; it is a pathway to greater awareness and appreciation of the world around us. As you sit quietly, hearing the chirps of the birds, you find yourself part of something larger, a witness to the delicate balance of life that sustains us all.

Take a Hike

Imagine stepping onto a trail where the morning light filters through the trees, casting dappled patterns on the path ahead. The air is crisp and invigorating and carries the scent of earth and pine. This is the world of hiking and walking in nature, a realm where fitness and fun intertwine seamlessly. As you move, each footstep is an opportunity to soak in the fresh air, a natural elixir that boosts both body and mind. Breathing deeply, you feel the stress of everyday life dissolve, replaced by a sense of calm and clarity. The natural environment acts as a balm, lowering stress levels and reducing anxiety, leaving you refreshed and rejuvenated.

Walking and hiking are more than just activities; they're gateways to physical health. Whether you're taking a leisurely stroll along a gentle path or challenging yourself with a rugged trail, these simple movements offer immense benefits. Your heart pumps stronger, your muscles work in harmony, and your endurance builds with each step. It's a workout tailored to your pace, improving cardiovascular health without the need for intense exertion. And the best part? Nature provides the backdrop, making exercise feel less like a chore and more like an adventure. As you traverse paths lined with wildflowers or shaded by towering trees, you're reminded that fitness can be a joyful part of everyday life.

When selecting parks and trails, it's essential to consider your fitness level. Think of it as choosing the right book to read—some trails are like light-hearted novels, easy and enjoyable, while others resemble epic tales filled with challenges and rewards.

What to look for - Beginner-Friendly Trails:

- **Flat Terrain:** Look for trails with minimal elevation gain. Paved or well-maintained gravel paths are ideal.

- **Short Distance:** Start with short trails (1-3 miles) and gradually increase the distance as you gain experience.

- **Easy Access:** Choose trails that are easily accessible with parking and restroom facilities.

- **Well-Marked Trails:** Clear signage is essential for beginners.

- **Examples (General Types - research your area):** Nature trails in local parks, paved bike paths, sections of rail trails, and boardwalks through wetlands.

For those seeking a bit more excitement, trails with varied terrain offer a satisfying challenge. Accessibility is key, too. Many parks cater to different mobility levels, offering wheelchair-accessible paths and shorter routes for those who prefer a less strenuous walk. This ensures that everyone, regardless of ability, can connect with nature in a way that suits them.

Parks and trails are not just about the paths you walk; they're about the experiences you gather along the way. Guided nature walks, for instance, open up a world of learning and exploration. Led by knowledgeable guides, these walks reveal the hidden stories of the landscape, from the flora and fauna to the history that shaped the land. It's like having a personal storyteller as you wander, adding depth and meaning to your outdoor adventures. Many parks also offer volunteer opportunities, inviting you to engage in clean-up days, conservation projects, or educational events. Through these activities, you not only give back to nature but also become part of a community dedicated to preserving the beauty of our natural spaces.

Exploring diverse landscapes is one of the great joys of hiking. Local parks and reserves offer a wide variety of environments to explore, each with its own unique character. You might find yourself wandering through wooded forests one day, then strolling by serene lakesides the next. These varied settings provide a feast for the senses, offering new sights, sounds, and experiences with every visit. And as the seasons change, so too does the landscape. Spring brings a burst of life as flowers bloom and birds sing. Summer bathes the world in warmth and light. Autumn paints the trees with vibrant hues, and winter transforms the land into a peaceful, snow-covered wonderland. Each season offers its own magic, inviting you to witness nature's ever-changing beauty up close.

Rediscovering local gems is a delight that often accompanies these outings. Many retirees find unexpected joy in uncovering hidden trails or scenic spots they never knew existed. It's a quiet creek where you can sit and listen to the gentle flow of water or a mountain overlook that offers breathtaking views of the valley below. These discoveries add a sense of adventure to your walks, turning each outing into a treasure hunt filled with moments of awe and wonder. It's a reminder that beauty often lies just beyond the familiar, waiting to be found by those willing to explore.

Nature walks and park activities are also excellent for building social connections. Joining group hikes or participating in park events allows you to meet like-minded individuals who share your love for the outdoors. As you walk and talk, sharing stories and experiences, friendships blossom naturally. These connections enrich your life, creating a network of friends who can accompany you on your adventures. Together, you celebrate the joys of nature, finding company and support in the shared pursuit of health, happiness, and discovery.

Be the Change

In today's world, the need for environmental stewardship is more pressing than ever. As someone who has witnessed the many changes in our environment over the years, I believe it's critically important to protect and preserve our natural world for future generations. Engaging in local conservation projects offers a tangible way to contribute to sustainability. These initiatives often involve efforts like habitat restoration, tree planting, or river clean-ups. By participating, you help ensure that parks, forests, and rivers remain vibrant and healthy, providing a nurturing home for wildlife and a beautiful landscape for everyone to enjoy. Your actions can make a difference, leaving a lasting positive impact on the environment.

Citizen science projects present another exciting opportunity to contribute to scientific studies and research efforts. These projects rely on volunteers to collect data, which scientists use to better understand and protect our natural world. Whether you're tracking butterfly migrations, monitoring water quality, or counting bird populations, your contributions add valuable information to ongoing research. Citizen science not only empowers you to play a role in scientific discovery but also deepens your connection to the environment. As you observe and document the world around you, you'll gain a greater appreciation for its complexity and beauty. It's a chance to learn, engage, and make a meaningful difference in the communities and ecosystems that surround us.

Getting involved in environmental initiatives is easy. Many local organizations host volunteer events, inviting community members to join efforts to protect and restore natural spaces. These events are often publicized through community centers, libraries, and online forums, making it simple to find opportunities that align with your interests. By volunteering for clean-ups or conservation projects, you not only contribute to a healthier planet but also become part of a community of like-minded individuals who share your passion for the environment. Working alongside others, you'll experience the company and the satisfaction that comes from working toward a common goal.

Finding Citizen Science Projects:

- **SciStarter:** This website is a hub for citizen science projects across various disciplines, including environmental science. You can search by location or interest.

- **Zooniverse:** This platform hosts a variety of citizen science projects, many of which involve analyzing images or data related to environmental research.

- **iNaturalist:** A platform for recording observations of plants, animals, and other organisms. Your observations can contribute valuable data to ecological research.

- **eBird:** If you're interested in birdwatching, eBird is a great platform for recording bird sightings and participating in bird conservation efforts.

- **Local Universities and Research Institutions:** Check with local universities or research institutions to see if they have any citizen science projects related to environmental research.

- **Government Agencies:** Agencies like the EPA, NOAA, and USGS often have citizen science initiatives related to environmental monitoring or data collection.

Beyond the hands-on activities, environmental initiatives often provide learning opportunities through workshops and educational seminars. These events cover a wide range of topics, from sustainable gardening practices to the latest in conservation technology. Attending these sessions allows you to expand your knowledge and stay informed about critical environmental issues. You'll learn practical tips for reducing your ecological footprint, discover ways to incorporate sustainability into your daily life and gain insights into how you can continue to support environmental goals. These workshops not only educate but also inspire, motivating you to take further action in protecting our planet.

Through environmental initiatives, you have the chance to be a part of something larger than yourself. Your efforts contribute to a global movement focused on protecting and preserving our planet for future generations. It's about acting and making a difference, no matter how small, in the pursuit of a healthier world. By participating, you not only shape the environment but also enrich your own life, finding purpose and fulfillment in the knowledge that you are leaving a positive legacy for those who follow.

Wrap-Up: A Final Word on Nature's Gifts

Imagine standing on the edge of a vast meadow, the horizon stretching before you, inviting you to explore its hidden treasures. This is what embracing the great outdoors feels like, an open invitation to discover the wonder and fulfillment nature offers. Throughout life, nature has been a steadfast companion, providing solace, inspiration, and joy. Now, in retirement, its gifts are more pronounced, offering countless opportunities for growth and connection. As you venture outside, you tap into a wellspring of vitality that nurtures not just the body but the mind and spirit as well. The simple act of stepping outdoors, breathing in the fresh air, and feeling the sun on your skin can transform an ordinary day into an extraordinary experience.

Outdoor activities have the power to enrich your life in profound ways. They offer a gentle form of exercise that keeps your body agile and your muscles strong, all while surrounded by the beauty of nature's landscape. Whether you're hiking forest trails, paddling along a tranquil river, or simply enjoying a stroll, these moments of movement invigorate your senses and elevate your mood. The natural world, with its vibrant colors and soothing sounds, serves as a backdrop to your adventures, enhancing each experience and grounding you in the present moment.

Mentally, time spent in nature can be a balm for the soul. The rhythmic patterns of the natural world, from the ebb and flow of the tides to the rustle of leaves in the wind, create a sense of harmony that calms the mind and reduces stress. In these moments of quiet reflection, you can find clarity and perspective, a chance to step back from the bustle of life and reconnect with what truly matters. Nature invites you to slow down, pause, and appreciate the simplicities of life that often go unnoticed. This mindfulness fosters a deeper connection to the world around you, nourishing your spirit and overall well-being.

Socially, the outdoors provides a unique platform for connection and community. It's a place where friendships are forged over shared experiences and common interests. Whether you're joining a local hiking group, participating in a community garden, or attending a nature workshop, these activities bring people together, creating connections that grow your social life. Engaging with others in outdoor settings fosters a sense of belonging and fellowship, reminding you that you're part of a larger community. These interactions not only expand your circle of friends but also offer opportunities for learning and growth as you share knowledge, stories, and laughter with those around you.

The gifts of nature are limitless, offering something for everyone. Nature invites you to explore new paths, discover hidden talents, and develop meaningful connections. As you continue this journey, may it be a reminder of the beauty and resilience of life, a testament to the wonders of our planet. Let nature be your guide, your teacher, and your inspiration. Embrace its gifts and allow them to lead you to a life of adventure, discovery, and fulfillment. As we conclude this book, the journey continues with new opportunities to enrich your life and explore the endless possibilities that await.

Conclusion

As we come to the end of this incredible journey, I want to reflect on all the fantastic possibilities we've explored together. From rediscovering your passions to building new social connections, this book has been a roadmap for navigating the exciting world of retirement. We've covered so much ground, from finding purpose and staying active to embracing lifelong learning and reconnecting with nature. It's an honor to share these ideas with you, and I hope they've sparked a sense of excitement and empowerment as you embark on this new chapter.

Remember, retirement is a time to invest in yourself. Keep learning, stay active, and prioritize those social connections that bring joy and meaning to your life. Whether it's pursuing a new hobby, volunteering for a cause you care about, or simply taking a daily walk in the park, each step you take is an opportunity to nurture your body, mind, and spirit. The key is to engage in those activities that genuinely resonate with you, the ones that make you feel alive and fulfilled.

So, my friend, here's my challenge for you: choose one thing from this book that excites you, and take that first step today. It could be signing up for a class, reaching out to an old friend, or researching local volunteer opportunities. Whatever it is, don't wait. This is your time to take control and create the retirement experience you've always dreamed of. The journey is yours to design, and I do not doubt that you'll make a path that's uniquely your own.

As you navigate this new place, remember that you're in the driver's seat. Be proactive, stay curious, and embrace new experiences with an open heart. There will be moments of joy, laughter, and connection, as well as times of reflection and growth. Embrace it all, knowing that each experience is shaping a retirement that's vibrant, fulfilling, and authentically you.

Retirement is an adventure, a chance to explore uncharted territories and discover new parts of yourself. Whether it's pursuing a lifelong passion, nurturing deeper friendships, or leaving a meaningful legacy, the opportunities to thrive are genuinely limitless. As you step into this exciting new phase, I encourage you to approach it with a sense of wonder and possibility. The world is your oyster, and there's no telling what incredible experience pearls await you.

On a personal note, thank you for joining me on this journey. As someone deeply passionate about helping people live their best lives, it's been a true privilege to share these ideas with you. I hope this book has served as a source of inspiration and guidance, and I hope it will help you accomplish much joy and happiness in the years ahead.

In fact, I had so many retirement suggestions to share that I divided the content into another book. I took care not to repeat any of the suggestions so each book can stand on its own, inspiring your retirement journeys.

As we close this chapter together, I want to leave you with a heartfelt thanks. Thank you for your time, your trust, and your willingness to explore these ideas with me. I wish you a retirement filled with joy, growth, and endless possibilities. May you embrace your newfound freedom with open arms and thrive in ways you never thought possible.

The adventure is just beginning, my friend. Here's to a retirement that exceeds your wildest dreams. Embrace the possibilities, and enjoy every moment of the journey ahead.

With gratitude and excitement for all that's to come,

Patti Gomas

Printed in Dunstable, United Kingdom

67221519R00077